Panzers on the Vistula

Panzers on the Vistula

Retreat and Rout in
East Prussia
1945

Hans Schäufler

Translated by
Tony Le Tissier

Pen & Sword
MILITARY

First published in German by Motorbuch Verlag in 1991 under the title
1945: Panzer an der Weichsel. Soldaten der letzten

First published in this translation in Great Britain in 2018 by
PEN AND SWORD MILITARY
an imprint of
Pen and Sword Books Ltd
47 Church Street
Barnsley
South Yorkshire S70 2AS

ISBN 978 1 52673 431 0

Printed and bound in England by
TJ International Ltd, Padstow, Cornwall

Typeset in Times by CHIC GRAPHICS

Pen & Sword Books Ltd incorporates the imprints of
Archaeology, Atlas, Aviation, Battleground, Discovery,
Family History, History, Maritime, Military, Naval, Politics,
Railways, Select, Social History, Transport, True Crime,
Claymore Press, Frontline Books, Leo Cooper, Praetorian Press,
Remember When, Seaforth Publishing and Wharncliffe.

For a complete list of Pen and Sword titles please contact
Pen and Sword Books Limited
47 Church Street, Barnsley, South Yorkshire, S70 2AS, England
E-mail: enquiries@pen-and-sword.co.uk
Website: www.pen-and-sword.co.uk

Contents

Foreword

Ernst W. Hoffmann

8032 Gäfelfing, 20. Febr. l980
Im Tann 1

The book '1945: Panzer an der Weichsel – Soldaten der letzten Stunde' is not only close to the truth, it is the truth! One cannot put it down until the last page.

Everyone experienced horrors: the explosive bombshells of the Soviet salvoes, the monstrous effect of massed enemy artillery, the uncountable bombing carpets of Allied enemy squadrons, the collapsed rows of buildings in Danzig, and the indescribable suffering of the poor, fleeing population – one experiences all this again in reading this book.

It really belongs in the hands of all adolescent boys, also in those of girls. Especially important for them is to learn about the fate of their parents and above all that of their mothers. It would be a worthwhile contribution to the better understanding of their parents' generation, because one has hardly read anything so detailed and vivid as this book describes until now.

Best wishes to this successful work!

Ernst W. Hoffmann, Colonel (Retd)
At that time Commander Panzergrenadier –
Regiment 12 and, following the death of General
Betzel, Commander of the 4th Panzer Division

Preface

This is no novel, no fabricated history, but a blunt factual account without embellishment, and without hatred.

Every name, every place, every detail is real, all events are true and at first hand, as seen with the eyes of 1945.

Much has already been spoken and written about the flight of the 2 million from East and West Prussia, but hardly anyone has mentioned that this, greatest rescue operation in human history, was made possible by the commitment of life and liberty of *THE SOLDIERS OF THE LAST HOUR*.

This book is written in memory of them.

Hans Schäufler, 1991

List of Maps

35. The Vistula is just over half a kilometre wide. Again and again Soviet fighter aircraft attacked the ferry.
36. In the late afternoon of 8 May 1945, the last day of the war, the ferry sailed.
37. On 27 May 1945, on the orders of the army, the locks on the Vistula were opened, flooding the Elbinger Werder.
38. Lieutenant-General of Panzer Troops Dietrich von Saucken, commander of the 2nd Army.
39. Lieutenant-General Blemens Betzel, commander of the 4th Panzer Division.
40. Colonel Ernst W. Hoffmann, commander of the 12th Panzergrenadier Regiment.
41. Colonel Hans Christern, commander of the 35 Panzer Regiment.
42. Hans Schaüfler, the author of this book.

Maps

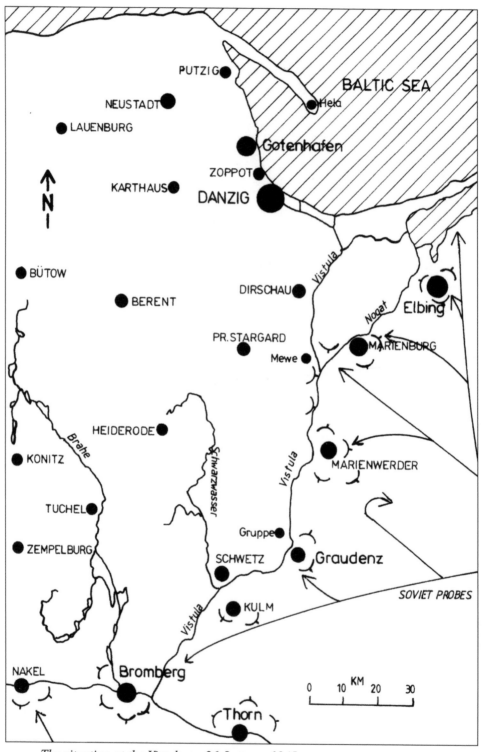

The situation at the Vistula on 26 January 1945.

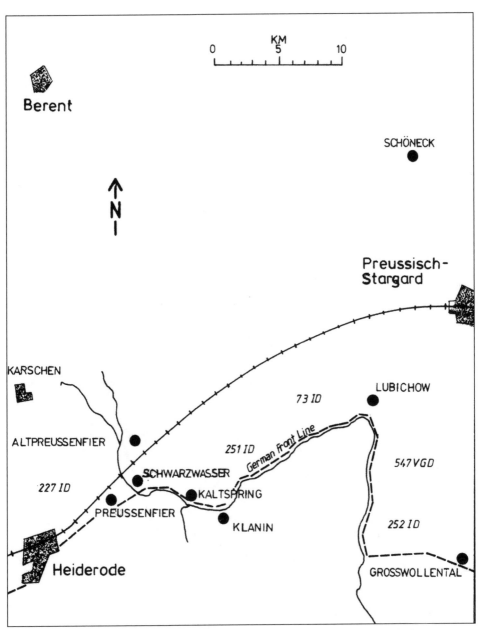

The situation between Heiderode and Preussisch Stargard on 21 February 1945.

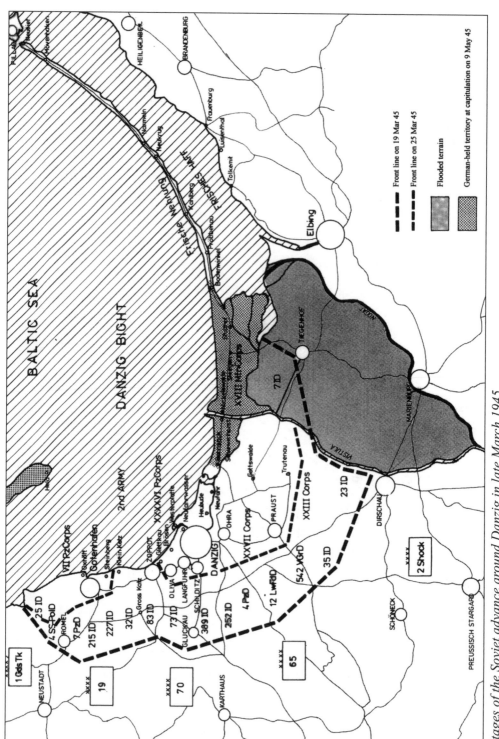

Stages of the Soviet advance around Danzig in late March 1945.

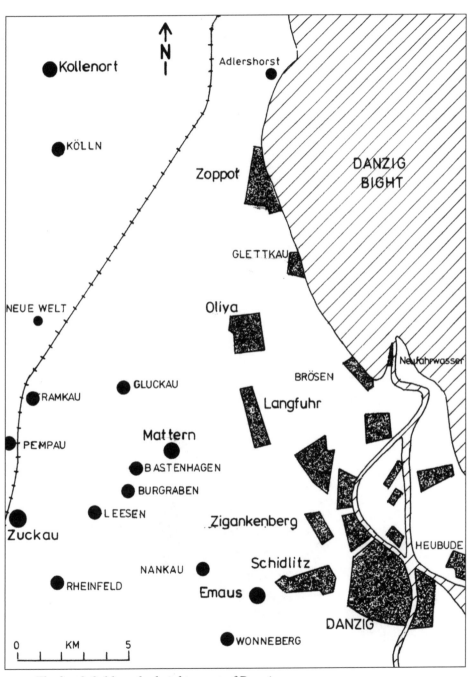

The battlefield on the heights west of Danzig.

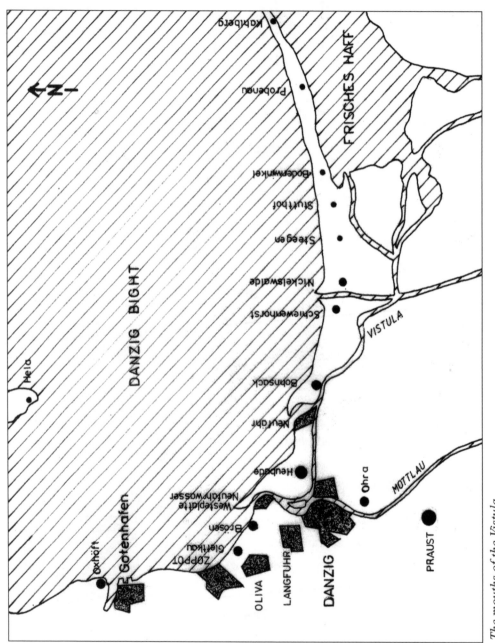

The mouths of the Vistula.

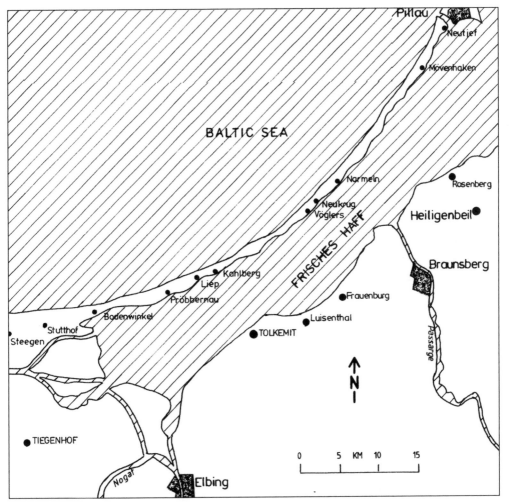

The Frisches Haff Lagoon from Steegen to Neutief.

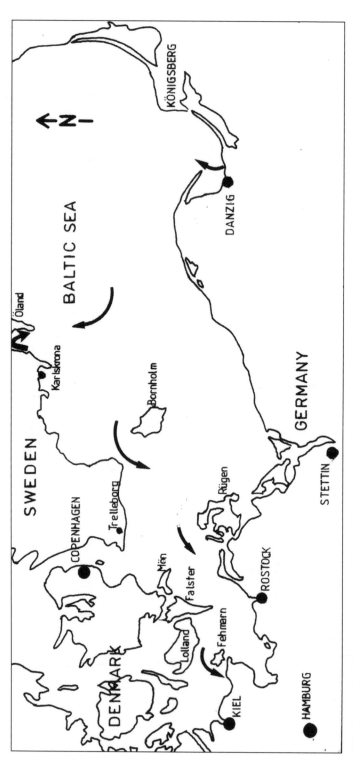

Flight over the Baltic.

Chapter 1

From Kurland to Danzig

The great Soviet Christmas Offensive, later dubbed the 3rd Kurland Battle, broke out in Latvia on 9 January 1945, I was then Second-Lieutenant and Regimental Signals Officer of Panzer Regiment 35, when an Army order was received that our 4th Panzer Division was to withdraw from the front near Dzukste and assemble in the Frauenburg area 'to refresh and prepare for action', as an order from Corps put it.

Because of the critical fuel situation, a risky move by rail was ordered even for this relatively short journey. Consequently, special anti-aircraft protection had to be established at the loading station of Biksti, which was close to the front, and as Soviet air superiority was so overwhelming. Nevertheless, it all went quickly and without incident, and early on the morning of 10 January the first train reached Frauenburg. When the Divisional move was complete on 16 January, orders were given to prepare to move again.

On 17 January a brief order came from Army Group Nord: 'The 4th Panzer Division will entrain immediately at Frauenburg station for embarkation at Libau. The 4th Panzer Division will leave behind all vehicles and heavy weapons when it leaves Army Group Nord.'

We were all delighted to turn our backs on the Kurland pocket, but this haste made us suspicious. Graudenz in West Prussia was given as our destination. According to the Wehrmacht Report, the Red Army had started its anticipated main offensive on Germany at the Vistula and Narev rivers on 12 January. The situation was unpleasant and made one apprehensive.

While we made our way to the new battleground with mixed feelings, an instinctive review of the fighting in Kurland was pressing.

On 10 August 1944 we had been released from the central section of the front east of Warsaw and hastily transported to Latvia, where we were tasked with re-establishing the disrupted land connection to Estonia and Army Group Nord, south of Riga, which had been cut off.

Heavy offensive fighting near Autz and Doblen ensued, until finally on 6 September the connection with Army Group Nord was achieved east of Tukkum and withdrawal to Latvia became possible. But then on 8 October, the Red Army's 1st Baltic Front broke through to the Baltic near Memel and severed the land connection a second time. This resulted in the formation of the 'Kurland bridgehead', which could only be reached and supplied by sea.

Three Soviet armies had thrust into Lithuania with a view to rolling up the German units cut off in Kurland from the south. The goal of the Soviet offensive was Libau, the traffic junction on the Baltic with its important ice-free harbour, the main supply base for the German troops in Kurland.

By 16 October Army Group Nord had drawn up detailed plans for the German troops to break through to East Prussia and preparations had begun. On 24 October the first German units attacked south, broke through the Russian positions and overran their belts of anti-tank guns. But this undertaking, which had begun so successfully, had to be broken off when the first big defensive battle started in Kurland on 27 October. The Soviet Army began a several hours long barrage with 2,000 artillery pieces firing on the German positions along the whole 200km front line between Tukkum and Libau.

For four whole weeks the earth of Latvia shook under the blows of this violent battle. Smoke and flames enshrouded the bulwarks along the Baltic, but the Soviet plan shattered with heavy losses and the brave resistance of the German troops.

On 3 November the Wehrmacht High Command reported: 'The attempted Soviet breakthrough in the area east of Libau was thwarted by the exemplary staunchness of our troops, resulting in the destruction of 62 tanks. In all the enemy lost 1,144 tanks in the Kurland area during the month of October.'

The Soviets gave up first. A depressing silence lay over a land torn up by shells and bombs, slowly sinking in the rain and mud. Losses on both sides had been heavy. Our own troops were exhausted by the fighting.

And then on 25 November the Soviet divisions attacked the German lines again with an inconceivable amount of equipment, this time between Preekuln and the Venta River. Defensive fighting continued until 7 December, but the Soviets were unable to break through here either. This went down in military history as the 2nd Battle of Kurland.

In mid-December the land was covered in frost. The mud and morass that had brought the 2nd Battle of Kurland to a standstill froze hard overnight. Not only the rutted tracks but the meadows and fields became passable to tanks. Then came clear winter skies and the Soviet fighters and bombers brought the trenches and troops' accommodation under constant attack with bombs and cannon fire, the supply harbours of Libau and Windau being their main targets.

On 21 December the Soviet artillery put down a hurricane of fire on the 35km front either side of Frauenburg with 170,000 shells of all calibres. It seemed as if everyone would die under the Red Army's assault on our lines at 0900 hours with a first wave of twenty infantry divisions. 'Only those that were there can understand what the soldiers' went through', wrote General von Saukken in the history of the 4th Panzer Division.

The splitting apart of Army Group Nord was yet again the Soviet's main objective, wishing to break through on either side of the Frauenburg–Libau road.

The 3rd Battle of Kurland ended on 4 January with no palpable success for the Red Army, but the German troops had had to pay a high price in blood – and that in the defence of several square kilometres of a foreign country while the Western Allies conquered city after city in their homeland. Deep depression was widespread.

Thus, it came almost as a relief, an easing of tension, when we boarded the transport in Libau to return home to fight the last battle on German soil.

The first elements of the 4th Panzer Division and tank crews of Panzer Regiment 35 embarked on the troopship *Preussen*. Our regimental commander, Colonel Christern, with a small staff and signals unit, went ahead in a fast naval vessel to make a reconnaissance of the Gruppe Training Area near Graudenz and to report on how many and what heavy weapons and tanks had been set aside for us. We remained in constant radio contact with him, even while on the troop transport.

Right at the beginning of the embarkation we were spotted by Soviet reconnaissance aircraft, which gave us a bad feeling, but fortunately heavy, hanging clouds filled the heavens so that our anti-aircraft guns only had to engage occasionally, and the few bombs that were dropped fell into the sea on either side of the ship.

Escorting naval craft immediately gathered around us and we entered the wintry Baltic Sea with a strong escort. Light waves caused the *Preussen* to roll and the first tank men became seasick, but this was not over the railings, for all such structures had been removed. Only a few strong steel cables crossed the upper deck to be held on to should anyone slip while moving about, but there was little inclination to do so. Most of the men were jolly glad to be able to stretch out fully in the warm fug below decks. There was a terrible stink of oil and other things in the completely overcrowded cabins and gangways.

Minesweepers went ahead checking the channel, stopping from time to time. Other escorting vessels circled nervously around us, gave submarine alerts, dropped depth charges and ordered zig-zag courses. When lifejackets were issued there were only sufficient for a third of the men, and when it came to the allocation of lifeboats the situation was even worse. There were certainly three times as many people on board as the regulations allowed.

The route was very carefully managed so that the largest escort was concentrated at night as we passed the Soviet-occupied coastal strip by Memel. For us tank men, this uncustomary means of transportation on the stormy, mined and Soviet submarine-infested Baltic was definitely not to our taste. It was a good night when the ship's anti-aircraft guns did not have to fire so often. Occasionally they disturbed us while firing at high-flying bombers, which then quickly turned away as the shells exploded close under their wings.

At last we arrived in the bay of Danzig on the morning of 21 January. Our patience was once more subjected to a hard test as we had to wait for a long time before we could disembark.

'What one has long to wait for, will be good in the end!' For a short time it was very good indeed. We were accommodated in the luxurious seaside resort of Zopput in the plush rooms of what I believe was called the Savoy Hotel. It was already an eternity since we had last slept on a mattress and covered ourselves with a feather duvet. We were able to do this here and forget the war for several days, feeling like holidaymakers, strolling on the swept sands, going to the cinema and enjoying the comforts of life with the motto: 'Enjoy the war, comrades, peace will be frightful!'

The news filtered through from the front, the tidings whispered from mouth to mouth, and the official announcements of the Wehrmacht bulletins painted a gloomy picture.

Chapter 2

The Situation on the Vistula in Mid-January 1945

With the arrival of the frost, 200 battle-strong Soviet divisions began the long prepared for main offensive along the 600km of the Eastern Front on 12 January. They pushed back the seventy battered German divisions opposing them, overrunning some, and breaking in at decisive points on a wide front.

The gigantic, potent Soviet Union was in a position to engage its massed forces, its whole armed might on this front and to concentrate on vital points as it liked.

In contrast, the German armed forces in the East could only defend themselves with one arm tied behind their backs, as the other arm had to try and hold off the impetuous Western Allies. Apart from that, there were still German divisions in Norway and the Balkans and, in a complete misjudgement of the situation, Hitler had sent strong armoured units to Hungary.

An immense industrial potential worked undisturbed and flat out producing armaments for the overwhelming enemy, while the German centres of production were bombed to smithereens and the traffic and supply routes lay within range of enemy aircraft. Germany's raw material situation was catastrophic. The appeal for 'total war' and the catchword 'five to twelve' were hanging around one's neck. The cries of Goebbels' propaganda for ultimate victory and the rumours of wonder weapons were barefaced lies. Many thought that the time had long gone past 'five to twelve'.

It was therefore not surprising if the confidence of the commanders in the political leadership, that of the fighting front in the Wehrmacht High Command and its totally false analysis of events, was deeply shattered. The only thing to be done was to save the innocent victims of this senseless war from the vengeance of the Red Army stirred up by Soviet demagogues.

On 12 January the 1st Byelorussian Front attacked from its Vistula bridgeheads south of Warsaw towards Hohensalza-Gnesen-Posen, the Soviets in the first assault ripping apart the German defences along a width of 150km after a mighty artillery preparation.

On 13 January the 3rd Byelorussian Front opened up with 350 heavy batteries and Stalin-Organs on the northern section of the front and attacked East Prussia between the Masurian Lakes and the Kurischen Haff lagoon with 7 armies comprising 54 rifle divisions, 2 tank corps and 9 independent armoured units.

Next day, Sunday, 14 January, the central northern sector was attacked by the 2nd Byelorussian Front from the Narev-Bug triangle towards the mouth of the Vistula River. This involved another 6 armies with 54 rifle divisions, 6 tank corps, 1 cavalry corps and 9 independent armoured units. The German troops defended themselves desperately but were unable to withstand the pressure for long.

The fine winter weather enabled the enemy to exploit their overwhelming air superiority to the full. Bomber and fighter formations of both Soviet and American manufacture operated devastatingly against the disintegrating German front as well as the withdrawal and supply routes. Soviet ammunition expenditure was enormous.

Whatever withstood the Red Army's first assault was crushed by artillery fire and probing armour. This brought deep disquiet and uncertainty on the German front, causing it to collapse decisively. The German divisions fell apart and the emergency units formed from scattered elements and supply units were unable to close the gaps. Despite all their courage and self-sacrifice, they were unable to stem the vigorously attacking enemy.

The front disintegrated into individual points of resistance. All of these tried to re-establish a continuous line of defence, but failed, being prevented by Soviet tanks carrying infantry penetrating deep into the hinterland.

The vast superiority in numbers of the Red Army, its enormous firepower and unimpeded mobility over the frozen ground, the strength of its battle groups and, above all, the lack of our own reserves, brought feelings of helplessness and a deep depression among the German troops. In some places the retreat became a wild flight.

The civilian population behind the crumbling front had been left in uncertainty by the officials and offices of the Nazi Party on the orders of their Gauleiters, so had no idea of the great danger threatening them and still felt themselves secure behind the mined 'East Wall'. Thus when at about 1700 hours on 23 January a Soviet tank unit burst unexpectedly into the city of Elbing, it came as a staggering blow to the Party offices and officials. Soon afterwards the Soviets had strong forces standing on the Frisches Haff lagoon, thus severing the last land connection with East Prussia.

Chapter 3

Collecting Our Armour

For us tank men enjoying a false peace in Zoppot, it came like a blow to the head when a radio message arrived from our regimental commander: 'Soviet tanks penetrating the Gruppe Training Area. Heavy weapons, armoured personnel carriers and tanks available in limited numbers. Get the crews moving immediately!'

The general situation appeared threatening. The Soviets had already reached Tolkemit on the Frisches Haff and were near Marienburg, 50km southeast of Danzig. The cities of Graudenz, Thorn and Danzig had been declared fortresses. No, we didn't want to be rounded up in Zoppot by the military police and forced into an unfamiliar infantry role with an emergency unit, so to Gruppe!

The men of Armoured Reconnaissance Battalion 4 and Armoured Signals Battalion 79 were the first to race off to the south on 23 January, as they had brought their vehicles with them from Kurland. They were followed by the men of Panzergrenadier Regiments 12 and 13 and the sappers of Armoured Engineer Battalion 79. Between them went the men of our Panzer Regiment 35, Panzer Artillery Regiment 103, Tank-Hunting Battalion 49 and Army Flak Battalion 290.

On low-loaders, towing vehicles and trucks, both organised and stolen, we drove off south without delay through mud and snow, by day and by night, without rest and without stopping, keeping the Vistula to our left, past the almost endless column of refugees pressing north along all the roads and tracks.

The news of the massacre at Nemmersdorf on 20 October 1944 had been widespread. There the Soviet troops had mercilessly and cruelly murdered all the inhabitants remaining in the village. The people on the roads believed that there had been many Nemmersdorfs in East Prussia but that was the only known bloodbath because it had been retaken by the German armed forces, and because the circumstances enabled an international commission to witness the Red Army outrage.

We saw German people in flight for the first time. Our hearts bled for them. Convoys of children led by brave young women, nuns and Red Cross sisters; horse-drawn wagons with the sick and aged, women, women, women, wounded and even more wounded, distress!

And they all silently begged us with reproachful glances to keep the Soviets from them and not leave them in the lurch.

Exhausted, disappointed German soldiers stood in the way for a moment with clenched fists: 'Stupid fools! Prolonging the war!' And we too wondered whether we were doing the right thing in confronting the Soviets again in view of the hopeless situation. Occasionally we came across small groups of German combat troops attempting to set up defensive positions on the roadside with the last of their strength. And then we saw another refugee column of children, women, old folk and wounded with their imploring eyes.

Further south the villages were as if dead, with not a single soul remaining. Nobody wanted to fall into the hands of the Soviets. All sought protection from the German troops.

Only we, unsuspectingly coming from Kurland, were swimming against the rising stream of fleeing people, wanting to secure and protect their escape route and make their salvation possible.

The abandoned houses and apartments upset us unusually. There was no disorder anywhere, everything was just left as if the inhabitants had gone shopping. Further to the south the glow of burning villages lightened the ghostly semi-darkness of the winter night, clouds of smoke blackening the snow-filled skies by day. Distant shots came across the Vistula.

Individual German soldiers were wandering around aimlessly, their faces showing horror and uncertainty. They were glad to see us at last, even if we were driving in what they took to be the wrong direction, and more and more comrades were stumbling along with blood-encrusted bandages.

We eventually arrived at the weapons depot in the Gruppe Training Area near Graudenz ahead of the Soviets. A warrant officer and several elderly corporals administered and guarded the combat vehicles and heavy weapons that a whole mass of administrators, technical inspectors and paymasters had formerly assuredly justified their existence maintaining, but these 'fine fellows', the senior administrators, had long since taken to their heels.

It has to be said that the relationship between the front-line troops and the rear services had significantly deteriorated during the big retreat from Russia. While the front lines were manned ever more thinly from year to year, the base cities bulged with supply service offices, administrative staff, Party officials, specialists and people wanting to prolong the war, but who ran for the exit as soon as sounds of battle could be heard. Over time this had embittered the front-line soldiers, who classified these people 'jwd' for 'quite far behind'.

We took over what weapons and vehicles we needed with little formality. The old warriors sought our blessing and our signatures as quickly as possible in order to complete their last task in this war with dignity and decency.

No tank had a complete radio installation. Others had been unscrewed and 'organised' before us. All the radio batteries and transformers were missing, having been misused in the air raid shelters to provide lighting. Nor was there a drop of fuel in the tanks. This, according to the senior corporal of the guard unit, had been siphoned off to enable the horde of administrators to get out of the danger zone. There was no fuel at all to get our tanks into position.

So three cheers for our workshop commander, Captain Bruno Schalmat, who appeared at the last minute with a recovery tank so full of fuel canisters that we were able to move 30km. The tanks did not have far to go. The Soviet T-34s in their victorious rashness drove straight into the barrels of our tank guns and experienced a cold shower. Fourteen T-34s were left on fire in the very first contact.

This gave the newly assembled crews, who were not yet practised in the unfamiliar tanks, the courage to take on this completely hopeless and unequal battle with the Red Army. The carelessly advancing Soviets, however, still obliged us to be careful. On the other hand, the refugee columns kept some distance from the fighting, which each day brought them another dozen kilometres further north, and every day the Navy removed several thousand of them.

Against the Soviet Joseph Stalin tank our otherwise excellent 75mm L48 gun had little effect. Only a lucky strike could get through its strong armour. Captain Kästner, the commander of our 1st Battalion, was therefore tasked by Division to recover our Panthers from Kurland and bring them to Danzig quickly.

Naturally we did not imagine that we would be able turn the wheel of history, for even the dumbest long knew that the war was lost. We could perhaps slow down the Red Army divisions pressing forward so as to give the slowly moving columns of refugees a chance to reach the Baltic harbours of Gotenhafen and Danzig ahead of the Soviets, and also give the Navy the time to secure what they needed to bring these helpless individuals over the Baltic to safety. Our limited actions could only be wasp stings to the enormous mass of the Red Army.

While the defensive front along the Vistula between Dirschau and Bromberg took shape, a gap yawned in the south from Thorn to Schneidemühl. The situation there was completely unclear.

That is why in mid-January the 31st Infantry Division had been thrown in towards Thorn to reinforce the hard-pressed 73rd Infantry Division, and our 4th Panzer Division and the 32nd Infantry Division had been brought across from Kurland. But with the elements arriving in dribs and drabs it was not possible to establish a continuous front, but rather only an observation screen that could identify enemy thrusts and alert our defences. This tactical recipe resulted in the Soviet troops, in our combat area at least, only advancing step by step.

Those elements of the 4th Panzer Division coming from Danzig that should have gone to the Gruppe Training area for refreshing and re-equipping with new equipment were thrown into battle piecemeal as they arrived. They observed, protected and fought along a 25km strip from Schweiz to Zempelburg.

Since 23 January elements of Armoured Reconnaissance Battalion 4 had been in mobile defence either side of the Brahe River from Kulm to Nakel, the reconnaissance troops securing the northern flank along the Soviet breakthrough heading for Schneidemühl.

On 24 January the 2nd Battalion, Panzergrenadier Regiment 33 was put on alert and detached to Bromberg at the disposal of the town commandant.

The value of our contribution being recognised, on 25 January Armoured Reconnaissance Battalion 4 was allocated a number of eight-wheeled armoured reconnaissance vehicles equipped with Tatra diesel engines and armed with 75mm tank guns. This was a double gain for the troops as there was sufficient diesel fuel available for the moment. One tried to adapt the petrol engines for it too, mixing it with pure alcohol from a schnapps refinery, but the results were not very good.

Apart from this, our Armoured Reconnaissance Battalion received some new armoured personnel carriers, of which some were equipped with 75mm short-barrelled cannon, some with 20mm quick-firing cannon and some with mortars. The battalion had also been able to bring their Luchs with it from Kurland, which were fast and agile fully tracked armoured reconnaissance vehicles also equipped with 20mm cannon. Our Armoured Reconnaissance Battalion had never had such immense firepower before. Naturally, there was also another snag; there was no fuel for these vehicles and only little ammunition for the 20mm and 75mm weapons.

On 26 January units of Panzergrenadier Regiment 12 and Armoured Reconnaissance Battalion 4 were engaged against Soviet airborne troops 7km west of Kulm.

On 27 January Nakel and Bromberg fell into Soviet hands. There was bitter fighting around Marienburg and the Soviets crossed the Vistula near Mewe, 60km south of Danzig. The 2nd Battalion of Panzergrenadier Regiment 33, detached to Bromberg, fought its way back north to the German front after the fall of the city. Armoured Engineer Battalion 79 had been defending the coastal strip near Zempelberg for days.

Gradually, the command was getting a grip on events in West Prussia. But snowdrifts and fuel shortages hampered the mobility of the armoured units. Consequently, the newly allocated fourteen Hunting-Tanks IV could not be deployed, although they were urgently needed everywhere, and had to remain at the unloading railway station.

The 4th Panzer Division was supported by Tiger tanks in engagements with the super heavy Soviet Joseph Stalin tanks on 30 January, but their performance too was marred by the acute lack of fuel, and 75mm and 30mm ammunition for the hunting tanks, Luchs and the armoured personnel carriers.

On 1 February there was a deep enemy penetration in the 337th Volksgrenadier Division's sector near Schweiz, seriously threatening the 2nd German Army's deep flank. The time was now right for the allocated fourteen Hunting-Tank IVs waiting for fuel near Karlshorst. On the Corps' orders they were combined with a group of tanks and set against the enemy breaking through.

Chapter 4

Gaining Time

On 1 and 2 February all available forces of the 4th Panzer Division attacked southeast under the personal leadership of the divisional commander, General Betzel, against the enemy breaking through towards Oscha, west of Schweiz, between the 251st Infantry and the 337th Volksgrenadier Divisions, and this with two weak tank companies with only a few litres of petrol in their fuel tanks and a limited amount of ammunition.

War correspondent Robert Peonsgen took part in the attack and described it:

2ⁿᵈ February 1945 – There was a misty night outside. I was at the command post of Captain Küspert, who commanded the tanks of Panzer Regiment 35. A reconnaissance troop had gone ahead towards the Blondmin cemetery, having spotted a Soviet unit without being seen itself. The men of Panzergrenadier Regiment 12 carefully worked their way back again and were able to alert our sentries. We huddled in a slit trench. Far and wide there was nothing to be heard. The Soviet soldiers were making their way forward very carefully. Suddenly there was an explosion half left. One could clearly hear the muffled hammering of heavy machine guns. An anti-tank gun barked in between and a mortar banged. The wild firing lasted for five minutes, then all was dead quiet again. A runner arrived bent over at the command post: 'Enemy group dealt with, one prisoner.' The Red Army soldier was brought to Captain Küspert. He was wounded and was first bandaged properly by us. He was hungry and we gave him bread, a cigarette and a glass of schnapps. Then he brightened up and gave us a big speech that we could not understand. He was taken back to the regimental command post in the vehicle that brought us hot coffee.

A few wounded from Panzergrenadier Regiment 12 hobbled

in, the last one a youngster leaning heavily on a stick. He fell down heavily on the straw in the room lit by several Hindenberg lights. We could see that he was biting his lips together and pointing to his trousers that were soaked in blood. We carefully pulled them off him. In his thigh was a hole big enough to put a fist in. He must have lost a lot of blood, but he was astonishingly brave. While the others bandaged him, I held his head and spoke to him gently to establish a rapport. He was not yet 18 years old and this had been his first action.

'That it would go so quickly, I would not have believed. I have seen nothing of the war!' That seemed to be his biggest pain, poor chap! He asked me if the wound was serious and he wanted to see it. We persuaded him not to, for the deep hole in his flesh looked ghastly. He was certainly upset with us.

As he was being bandaged, he complained about the pain in his left leg. We examined him further and found a second deep wound on the left side of his leg, which, however, did not look life endangering. Only a normal amount of flesh was missing. With all this misfortune, the youngster had had a tremendous stroke of luck – and we told him – and wished him all the best at home – he came from Ingolstadt.

I then slept for a while, sitting on some junk, my head against a large stone jar filled with salted meat that was however off and stank terribly. Nevertheless, I was so tired that I missed Captain Küspert's return and only awoke when everyone went outside. It was already dawn and the attack was due to begin in half an hour.

I reported to Captain Küspert as a war correspondent and asked him if I could ride with him in his command tank, which had a fixed turret and a dummy gun barrel. I felt horrible and could not eat anything. The tank slowly pushed through the gardens to the start point. At 0800 hours the tanks broke out of the edge of the wood onto the railway line towards Blondmin from the positions they had taken up during the night and rolled at breakneck speed over the snow-covered fields. Heavy defensive fire came from the village. We watched the attack in cover from behind a hedge with our binoculars. Captain Küspert sat on the edge of the turret and gave his orders to fire over the radio, as we could clearly see the anti-tank gun positions from the flash coming from their muzzles. Our tanks were also firing like mad into the village, which was starting to burn in several places.

One black dot after another appeared on the open fields. These were the Soviet mortar hits that marked the snow with black smoke powder.

And gun smoke lay like a thick fog over the fields and meadows, drawn from the garish muzzle flashes. The Panzergrenadiers followed the rolling panzers in thin waves. Here and there one saw one or two jump up run a few paces then fall back in the snow. A few kept lying there.

As the outermost left wing reached the village, Captain Küspert ordered his right wing to attack. The tanks pushed forward out of their cover, the Panzergrenadiers with them.

I was secretly hoping that the captain would stay here, where we had good cover between the buildings, but he was no 'long-distance commander'. Our vehicle, on whose back I was standing, pushed forward growling and swaying to the forward edge of the bushes. There was a small church behind us. We too now came under heavy fire. One heard quite clearly the bang of the anti-tank gun, but could not see if it was firing at us or something else. Heavy mortar bombs banged into the buildings behind us, sending the slates and red dust flying through the area.

One of our tanks, 50m away from us, was hit in the side. Then came an ear-deafening bang. I had long since made myself small behind the turret, pressing myself to the back like a bug. Captain Küspert, who was still with the whole of his body exposed above the turret, vanished with a crash like greased lightning, only one arm still sticking out. For a moment it was quite dark around me. Lumps of snow and clods of earth came down like hail and splinters banged against the steel. There was a shot through my glove a millimetre from the forefinger. A 122mm shell had exploded half a metre from our right-hand driving wheel.

We got up again and moved close to the church. Another piercing blow, a clattering and crash, as the church was hit 10m away. I was smothered in pieces of red tile. Only the adjutant was now standing in the tank turret. Captain Küsper had been wounded, having ducked down quickly, but leaving his arm exposed, and had caught some splinters.

Our tank rolled further forward. The left wing was already involved in heavy street fighting. The Soviets were firing out of all the buildings. The right wing also moved in nearer and nearer to the fire raging within the village. Flames flared from the roofs and black smoke stood over the place.

Our command tank followed the others. We swung at speed across to the cemetery, which was churned up by shell hits, but no tank went over a grave, which was noticeable as the land around had been ripped up by tracks.

The artillery fire suddenly began to diminish. The Soviet batteries at the village exit had been silenced, only individual guns firing from further away could be heard, and the fire direction seemed confused as the shells were exploding randomly in the neighbourhood.

Then we too were standing at the entrance to Blondmin. The first of our own tanks showed up on either side of the village. We could see the abandoned Soviet guns, both anti-tank and infantry, with the naked eye.

We drove close by one of these positions. Our tanks had aimed well. The ground about was churned up from hits and the trees behind were shredded. Many dead lay in the snow and the guns were blasted together. The ammunition trucks were standing not far from the position, all American Studebakers.

The sound of fighting diminished in the village. We went forward a bit until we could see over the Ebensee lake. A super heavy Joseph Stalin was firing from there which our Panzer IVs were unable to deal with.

The Red Army soldiers tried to flee. Those trucks and guns that could not use the roads any more were stuck in the snow. The Soviets skedaddled over the open field on foot and on sledges, looking like black spots against the white snow.

Three of our own tanks that were still standing on the road near the forester's house now moved forward, rolling though the wood. At 1100 hours the important crossroads 20km northwest of Schweiz were attacked and taken. We were unable to watch the action from our position, so we drove back past the cemetery and came to the village.

The Panzergrenadiers had already got a few of the Russian-American trucks going and siphoned the valuable fuel from the others. However, we drove into the village, where there was some rich booty to be had, really good things that the Soviets must have left lying about. Most of it was looted German goods. There were masses of tins of fruit, fish, and meat, as well as cigars and cigarettes, everything the heart desired. There was cooked chicken on the tables in the village, the Soviets having slaughtered all the small livestock, but certainly without thinking that the Germans would return to eat it.

The fires crackled outside as we sat in front of steaming dishes and filled our stomachs, undeterred by the stench of Russian excreta in the corners.

After this 'snack' our tank rolled back along the main road through the woods towards the crossroads. We soon caught up with the leading tank. Two farms were burning sky high on the left, where the Soviets had again put up a resistance and engaged our tanks with heavy fire. We saw the wrecks of two T-34s and a self-propelled gun emitting pitch-black smoke.

Captain Küspert was briefed on the situation by the tanks' commanders and issued orders for the further attack. A group of tanks peeled off to the left while the tanks near us observed the edge of the woods and gave immediate fire support whenever resistance flared up. The tanks swung left as if on parade with fire and movement. Once they had crossed the road to Ebensee, they swung round in a wide curve to the burning farms on the right. We could make out the grenadiers dismounting and searching the buildings while the tanks followed, knocking down the fences and undergrowth.

We passed the crossroads and went past the other tanks and through the strip of woodland, which was clear of enemy. A security line was established here for the night.

Our attack had gained us a considerable amount of ground, especially forcing the Soviets to think again. But the action was not yet over. When our regimental commander, Colonel Christern, returned from a conference with the Divisional staff, he explained the situation to us. The Soviets had launched an attack with strong infantry and armour to the north from the west of the Vistula, with the aim of rolling up the front from the rear and cutting off the German forces still fighting east of the river.

The city of Thorn, which had been declared a fortress and surrounded for two weeks by the Soviets, now already lay 40km from the German lines, and had been abandoned. The brave garrison, mainly consisting of the 73rd and 31st Infantry Divisions, had not surrendered to the Soviets, but had broken out of its steel ring and was now approaching the German Vistula front like a wandering island of resistance, and was already in great danger at this point in time. It therefore had to be assisted quickly and with vigour.

Division had therefore ordered an attack for the next day to divert the Soviets eastwards to Julienhof and relieve the 542nd Volksgrenadier Division, in order to clear and hold open the line of retreat for the Thorn group.

At dawn on 5 February the armoured combat team of the 4th Panzer Division, to which all the Corps's fuel resources had been allocated, moved out of the Blondmin area. Despite heavy anti-tank fire, the intended goal was reached, but the group had to turn back at nightfall from Julienhof to the Ebensee because strong Soviet armoured units equipped with Joseph Stalin tanks had appeared in its rear.

Then on 4 February, Heavy Tank Battalion 664 was assigned to the Division's support, and it was able to gain more ground to the east and even hold it on 5 and 6 February.

On 7 February the Thorn group was directed by radio to Schönau, 3km south of Schweiz, so as to break through to the German lines under cover of our attack.

On 8 February eighty men of the Thorn group were taken on the far left wing. Soviet resistance with artillery salvoes, ground-attack aircraft and mortars was enormous.

On 10 February our 4th Panzer Division attacked two Soviet infantry divisions with about fifty tanks in the sector comprising some 40km extending from Oscha to Zempelburg. Soviet ground-attack aircraft engaged every movement and disrupted the sensitive lines of supply. Above all, Tuchel railway station was their almost constant target.

Finally, finally, on the night of 10/11 February the remains of the Thorn garrison reached the German lines. In the history of the 4th Panzer Division, General von Saucken, the later commander-in-chief of the 2nd Army, praised the performance of elements of the 73rd and 31st Infantry Divisions: 'That this brave little band was able to reach the German lines deserves the highest recognition. This achievement was only possible by holding tightly together with a firm determination not to be taken prisoner.'

From 12 February the equipment of the fighting troops improved dramatically. All the companies of the 1st Battalion, Panzergrenadier Regiment 12 were able to be equipped with armoured personnel carriers, including even the regimental headquarters and signals platoon.

Our Panzer Regiment 35 had already for some time been allocated Panzer IVs and Jagdpanzer IVs, and Panzer Artillery Regiment 103 the guns that had been lacking.

However, the personnel situation remained catastrophic. The division had received 400 reinforcements, but the casualties had been enormous. For instance, on 11 February the combat strength of the 1st Battalion, Panzer Regiment 33, consisted of only twelve men, all totally exhausted, and these men had a 12km sector of the front to defend. This was why a continuous defensive front was impossible. The connection with the 32nd Infantry Division, which had come from Kurland at the beginning of February and was deployed west of our 4th Panzer Division, was lost.

The Soviets' intentions showed up clearly. Day and night their bombers and ground-attack aircraft attacked the railway stations at Tuchel and Könitz, crippling the railway connection. Our 4th Panzer Division had the primary task of preventing a Soviet breakthrough to Tuchel, for, in view of the acute fuel shortage, the troops were dependent upon the railway for supplies. Of course, the Soviets knew this too.

The battle for Tuchel surged back and forth. Because of the lack of personnel, the defence was only possible by using small strongpoints. The Soviets' tanks broke through between these strongpoints carrying infantry again and again, threatening the defenders from the rear. A radio message from Armoured Reconnaissance Battalion 4 on the evening of 12 February demonstrated the then uncertain situation and also the determination to hold the enemy: 'Back to Oswalden. All-round defence with straggler elements.'

The 389th Infantry Division, newly introduced via Danzig, was deployed in the gap between the 32nd Infantry and 4th Panzer Divisions in their support. The front crumbled here and there, but a radio message provided the new strength with which to hold on: '7th Panzer Division on its way!'

The railway station at Tuchel, so important for re-supply, had to stop working on 13 February as it was not only under constant fire from Soviet ground-attack aircraft, but also now under coordinated fire from enemy mortars and rocket launchers. No further supply trains could be unloaded and no wounded entrained. A bold counterattack by the 32nd Infantry Division west of us brought some relief, especially south of Könitz, but now the connection to the east with the 227th Infantry Division was severed. A counterthrust by our Panzer Regiment 35 re-established contact, but the rage of the Soviet attacks continued on 14 and 15 February. The German ranks thinned out more and more in comparison with the enemy superiority in materiel. To avoid street fighting and the unbearable casualties involved, Tuchel was evacuated on the night of 14/15 February without a fight.

The harshness of this struggle to win time is perhaps shown by the scores. The 4th Panzer Division alone in this period from 10–14 February destroyed 99 enemy tanks, 12 assault guns, 2 armoured cars and 41 anti-tank guns in the Tuchel area.

However, what was far, far more important was that it considerably slowed down the Red Army's advance northwards, prevented their breaking through and won valuable time for the refugees to make their way to the Baltic harbours and transportation to Schleswig Holstein. Unfortunately, they also suffered considerable losses from the constant attacks by Soviet ground-attack aircraft and bombers.

On 16 February the German defensive front ran about 3km north of Tuchel and connections east and west had been restored. A short break had done all of us good.

Armoured Reconnaissance Battalion 4 defended Könitz on its own until 16 February and was then relieved by the arrival at last of the 7th Panzer Division, which was able to continue to hold on to the place for another two days.

On 18 February, Captain Kästner reported from Danzig the arrival of twenty-seven Panthers from Kurland and a further detachment of twenty-three Panthers from the administrative net. The Panther, also known as the Panzer V, was a heavy tank of the latest construction with a 700hp engine and a very accurate 75mm tank gun that could take on a Joseph Stalin. The allocated tanks arrived by train at Kardien via Heiderode on 24 February.

The 1st Battalion of our Panzer Regiment 35, commanded by Captain Kästner, which had also been fully equipped with Panthers in Kurland, was reequipped with these. We were now again an almost war-strong tank regiment with two battalions and a fire and fighting strength seldom equalled before.

As it was to be expected that the two battalions would be separated and sent to different danger points, the voice ultra-shortwave radio apparatus having a range of only 10–15km, a regimental command tank was allocated to both. Next to the ultra-shortwave set, these tanks had an 80-watt middle-wave set of considerably longer range. Colonel Christern climbed with his command group into a radio armoured personnel carrier in which I was also located.

Our 4th Panzer Division was let loose and assigned in combat teams to the army's counterattack reserve. We feared that elements of our

Panzer Regiment 35 would be assigned to individual groups and infantry units, as often experience had shown that these valuable weapons were often not used effectively.

Chapter 5

From Tuchel to
Preussisch Stargard

We now had the chance to check our technical equipment. Then, on 20 February, the Soviets attacked the 251st Infantry Division east of Heiderode with strong forces and hit it so hard that it was completely shaken, as Corps stressed.

Captain Kelsch's combat team stormed into the corresponding gap in the front line with concentrated firepower against the attacking Soviets and hit them at the exact moment they were crossing the bridge by Kaltspring. The Soviets were pushed back with heavy losses and the bridge blown, thus making it possible to repel all later enemy attacks.

In the meantime, Colonel Hoffmann's combat team hit the Soviets in the rear and reoccupied Klanin.

In a further counterattack on 21 February the severed link to the 73rd Infantry Division was re-established and the 251st Infantry Division withdrawn into a defensive position.

In combination with our tanks, the Hoffmann combat team thrust southwest as far as Preussenfier from Schwarzwasser. A new engagement southwards from Karschen on the same afternoon with the 2nd Battalion, Panzer Regiment 35, Armoured Reconnaissance Battalion 4 and the 1st Battalion, Panzergrenadier Regiment 12, again under the command of Colonel Hoffmann, retook Guternwirt and Schöndorf, west of Heiderode, thus closing the gap in the front line.

On 22 February another enemy breach in the 251st Infantry Division had to be eliminated by Armoured Reconnaissance Battalion 4, while one company was detached to the 73rd Infantry Division on instructions from Corps. Against the objections of the company commander, these armoured vehicles were deployed completely unsuitably in wooded country north of Habichtsdorf and without infantry escort. A fiasco ensued. Two of our own Panzer IVs were shot up by the Soviets before they could do anything.

On 23 February the Hoffmann armoured group had to go from Mühlheide to the aid of the hard-pressed 227th Infantry Division. Unfortunately, this also showed no understanding of how tanks have to fight in units, as the orders reveal: 'Two Panzer IVs with a grenadier platoon to the neighbour on the right. Three Panzer IVs and one assault gun to Height 147 to strike at Kolonie Long. Two Panzer IVs to secure the railway line south of Alt-Preussenfier.' The result was that by the evening of 23 February only eight tanks of this armoured unit were still fit for combat.

'Don't dilute, concentrate!' was Colonel-General Guderian's motto, but despite all experience this was ignored.

Tanks were now highly technical fighting vehicles with sensitive, easily disrupted apparatus and instruments requiring constant attention and care. The least damage in battle could lead to fatalities and the loss of valuable tanks. Lack of technical understanding about their use and limitations, partly through egoistic and narrow thinking with in some cases even the brutal use of force, led to their allocation to non-motorised units, often to losses and failures, which were later made the fault of the tanks' crews. Consequently, every tank commander shuddered when he heard of an attachment to the infantry.

Since 1 February our Panzer Regiment 35 had been in constant action at the critical points in the fighting without a chance of attending to and checking its equipment. Much avoidable damage had thus been incurred and the number of fully combat-ready tanks had been sharply reduced. A further hindrance was the permanent scarcity of fuel and ammunition.

Nevertheless, we had to carry on without a rest, always ready to help out with the 73rd Infantry Division that had been decimated in Thorn, the badly chewed up 251st and the bruised 227th Infantry Divisions. Due to the constant 'fire brigade' actions in snow showers and on muddy ground, the troops were very overtired and weakened.

The 1st Battalion with its Panthers and Jagdpanzers was in action for the first time on 25 February. The bitter defensive fighting moved to the vicinity of Preussich Stargard and south of Berent.

Hermann Bix, sergeant-major and platoon commander in the 1st Battalion of Panzer Regiment 35, described his many engagements there:

We were extremely angry when we had to take over *Jagdpathers* instead of our usual Panzer Vs, which, in the general chaos, had failed to reach the self-propelled artillery battalion as expected.

Then we were forced to examine the equipment a bit closer. The tanks had no swivelling turret. One had to aim with the whole tank and one sat a little too much out in the open but, on the other hand, the steel monster disposed of a first class 88mm gun with enormous penetrating power, a fabulous range and great accuracy. So we quickly forgot the unusualness of the Jagdpather and made ourselves familiar with its advantages. We soon had the opportunity of exploiting them to the full.

It was the end of February 1945. I was located south of Preussisch Stargard with three of these Jagdpanzers, covering the withdrawal of the grenadiers and the construction of a new defensive front further back. Everything was going back, only the dark humps of earth retaining a light covering of snow indicating the abandoned German positions. I stood with my Jagdpanther in a little village behind a large dung heap in such a position that I could just see over it with my eyes, as could the gun. The flat turret of our tank only protruded a tiny bit over the cover.

Behind me stood Sergeant-Major Dehm with yet another Jagdpather, both of us having hardly any ammunition. Without shells he was only a nuisance to me. I signalled to him to move back a bit.

As the fog slowly lifted, two Soviet tanks appeared quite cautiously on a hill in front of us and felt their way slowly forward. When they came to within 1,200 metres I could see that they were neither T-34s nor KW-1s, but American tanks. From experience I knew that at this range they were comparatively easy to hit. We shot both on fire and for a while no other Ivan stuck his nose out.

A group of tank men were guarding the village, crews that had lost their tanks, so I was secure from surprises from right and left. One had a very limited view from the tank and anyway one cannot have one's eyes everywhere.

About half an hour after the shooting up of the two tanks I heard tank noises 1,000 metres further to the right and soon picked out two Soviet tanks trying to go round the village. My 88mm gun fired so accurately at this distance that there were no near-misses. Soon both tanks were burning.

It was obvious to me that the Soviets were seeking a weak point at which to break through. It was important to be alert along the whole front, as I was alone and out on a limb. The two other

Jagdpathers had pulled back with my consent as they had shot themselves out. My gun-aimer reported a stock of 5 explosive and 20 armour-piercing shells.

Second-Lieutenant Tautorus, my company commander, was somewhere around with his Panthers. I reported my position and lack of ammunition to him by radio, and received the order to hold back the Soviets as long as possible, as the infantry had not finished digging in.

Meanwhile the visibility had reduced to the extent that I was unable to observe everything happening to my right and left. The Soviets could have arrived marching in step and column of threes without having been noticed.

I observed the slope opposite closely and realised that the Soviets had openly brought two anti-tank guns into position. I loaded with explosive, gave my firing order and saw bits of wood and material flying in the air. Those lads had caught us out this way, had put a dummy into position and had locked onto our fire. Not stupid! And we fools had fallen for it! I was not going to fall for it a second time. I regretted my valuable shell.

I kept dead still, having my tank roll back a little so that we could not in any way be seen from the front. Only when I stuck my head out of the turret could I see straight over the cover. I could hardly believe my eyes. I saw a long column of tanks coming straight towards me, the leading one about 1,200 metres away, with supply trucks close behind the tanks.

I had previously divided the terrain in front of me into set points and carefully established the ranges, so I could reckon on hitting the leading tank with an armour-piercing shell when it reached the 800 metre mark.

I do not know why, but my superb gun aimer did not hit the tank with his first round, but a vast tree on the road edge. The trunk broke apart and the crown with its thick branches fell on the leading tank, which slipped, having suddenly lost its vision, and fell head over heels into the deep roadside ditch and lay motionless.

The following tanks closed up tight and stopped, not having identified me. They all turned their turrets to the right and fired like a fire brigade at the dark heaps of earth of the abandoned infantry position.

Then we joined in, and it was an easy game as I had the

broadsides of their turrets right in my line of fire. But we had to aim carefully, as we had so few shells. Even if an enemy tank survived after we had fired at it, things could turn nasty for us.

So I fired first at a tank in the middle of the column, which burst into flames with the first shot. Next came the tank at the rear, which also burst into flames. Then we fired effortlessly at the row, one after another, as they stood there like targets on the range.

Within ten minutes we had shot up eleven Soviet tanks in the column. The rest drove off in panic, trying to turn and getting stuck in the ditch, where they were wrapped in the flames and smoke from the long row of burning tanks.

I gave the order to fire at the trucks, but the gun aimer reported only two shells left. The machine gun ammunition had also run out. Now it was high time to disappear from the scene, for without ammunition even the best tank was useless.

We reversed slowly for the ground was weak with hardly any grip. Turning here was impossible. We could only move quite carefully backwards, metre by metre, withdrawing from sight of the column, which was now slowly coming to life.

The heavy engine of our tank howled loudly under the strain. We were only a few metres from solid ground, but the tracks churned away if the driver gave only a little more gas. Then I had an almighty shock. A Soviet tank was standing 300 metres right of us in the village. It had wound its way through unnoticed by us, wormed its way between the houses and apparently suspected no German tanks.

However, as it only could happen, he spotted us and I had to watch idly as he slowly turned his turret toward us. Unfortunately we could not do the same because of our fixed turret.

But then the Soviet tank remained still. I realised that without doubt that this was an unique opportunity to shoot. I screamed, no roared: 'Back and turn left! Stop! Turn right here!'

But our toboggan was standing in mud and moved only slowly, much too slowly. This made me nervous and my disquiet transferred itself to the crew. The gun-loader, who was the first to sense the danger, reminded me: 'Only two armour piercing shells!' My heart began to thump. It was something wonderful for me. We simply could not get into a firing position. Only the driver knew exactly what was up, as he had my order to get the tank into a firing position when he could.

I did not want to, but I had to realise that we would be unable to do it, as the steel colossus would only move a centimetre at a time in this mud bath, and the gun on the Soviet tank was pointing directly at us. Was I seeing right? Or was it a ghost? It was standing a bit too high!

Then a jolt went through my body. I was suddenly fully conscious again. I followed every movement by the Russian exactly, not missing the slightest detail. And then my opponent made a decisive error. The driver, believing he had time, wanted to bring his tank forward as its rear was too low, but it was sinking deeper and deeper as the ground there was also a morass.

Only seconds earlier I had been ready to give up: 'Hermann, make your peace with Heaven quickly. It will soon be all over!' But now I saw a chance for us. 'Keep calm!' I told myself. Our tank turned slowly until we were in a firing position. The gun was clear and at the right height. The gun-aimer carefully took aim. Our opponent was sinking ever deeper by the stem and I saw how he was trying in vain to lower his gun.

Suddenly the turret hatch flew open and two hands stretched out and waved. Did the crew want to surrender? Or did they want to fool us. We were used to this sort of thing. No, I could take no risks. We fired our penultimate shell into the projecting side to cover every eventuality. The crew jumped out – one, two, three, four men – all in order.

Then the last shell thundered into the Soviet tank and it immediately burst into flames, the sixteenth that morning.

But now we had to go. A tank without ammunition in the sixth year of the war was worthless.

Yes, one needs luck in war, and eyes in one's head, and a Jagdpanzer, and a crew like this!

Note: Sergeant-Major Hermann Bix was the twenty-third member of Panzer Regiment 35 to be decorated on 22 March 1945 with the Knights' Cross of the Iron Cross for destroying seventy-five tanks in the eastern campaign.

Chapter 6

The Race to Danzig

On 4 March the 4th Panzer Division was suddenly ordered to change its area of operations from Heiderode to Bütow, 50km away, in order to assist the 32nd Infantry Division.

Panzer Regiment 35 was already engaged in heavy fighting on 5 March near Gross-Tuchen, 12km south of Bütow where, according to the orders from Corps, their own infantry were hardly able to hold on. The regiment's tanks shot up twelve Soviet tanks and an assault gun. The two neighbouring divisions to the west could be seen to be retreating. The front was breaking up.

In this critical situation an Army order was received by the 4th Panzer Division at 2330 hours on the 5th: 'Assignment of an armoured combat team by rail to Damerkow, six kilometres west of Bütow; commander Colonel Christern.' The situation must have worsened dramatically. We had no idea at this time that the Red Army's spearheads had already reached the Pomeranian Baltic coast near Köslin and cut off our 2nd Army from the homeland, and that our re-supply was now only possible by sea.

The Christern group was released at 0600 hours on 6 March and got ready for a move by rail at Bütow. It consisted of the 1st Battalion, Panzer Regiment 12, and all available armoured vehicles of Panzer Regiment 35. Only the Jagdpanzer IVs had to remain behind.

In accordance with orders from Corps, all wheeled vehicles had to gather in the area Bukowin-Sierakowitz-Mirchau. These orders did not sound good at all: 'The 4th Panzer Division is about to move a long distance. We cannot bank on sufficient fuel for all the vehicles. The new combat area is around Neustadt in West Prussia.'

They travelled using small amounts of fuel taken from indispensable, essential vehicles like field kitchens, and ambulances that could be found at Bütow railway station on the afternoon of 6 March. We did not let the vague plans trouble us too much.

It was snowing as the train left Bütow railway station at 0900 hours.

Visibility got worse and worse. It also had its advantages, as we were safe from the Soviet fighters and bombers. But we moved into this milky murk with mixed feelings. The situation was uncertain. Nothing was known about the enemy. There was no longer any air reconnaissance, not even one close reconnaissance from the reconnaissance battalion, as it had no fuel. And there were hardly any prisoner interrogations available.

It was therefore ordered that all vehicles would be manned during the journey, their weapons ready for action, and that it would perhaps be necessary to go straight into action from the train. All radios were on 'Receive' but strict radio silence had to be observed, which meant no transmissions were to be made so as not to betray our move and current situation to the Soviets listening in and their radio direction finding units. The tanks' smoke dischargers were checked so that if the transport should be in danger they could be suddenly discharged.

The goods train moved slowly northwards, sometimes only at walking pace. The stations we passed through were unoccupied, deserted by the staff. There was nothing alive to be seen left and right of the tracks. The wagons crept through the snow flurries like a ghost train. The locomotive was set in the middle. Each tank on its open wagon had been given its precise observation and firing arcs. Unloading apparatus lay ready for use on every wagon. We had never before travelled like this during all the years of war.

We had fuel sufficient for 30km in our tanks and only a few shells in the racks. In short, the situation was drastic, the atmosphere poor. At this point in time no one knew exactly what was happening, or that those German forces still intact were involved in a fateful race to the Baltic with the Soviet divisions.

A radio message from Corps in the late afternoon poured fresh water on the rumour mill: 'Enemy has broken through XXIIIrd Corps and is marching on Danzig. Armoured combat team from 4th Panzer Division to prepare for action!'

During the darkness our train remained well covered in a railway cutting. As we were approaching Damerkow railway station, 25km southwest of Lauenburg, early on the morning of 7 March, we heard a radio message: 'Damerkow strongly occupied by the enemy.' Colonel Christern had the train stop so that we would not be seen from that place. We could hear the sound of fighting in the distance, but there was also a Damerkow between Bütow and Gross Tuchen that we had been talking about the day before. We had no idea, which of the two

Damerkows was on our railway line, but could not ask as radio silence still applied.

There was nothing else for the colonel to do but drop off his command tank and go and see for himself with his radio team, as he could not risk the train going on and becoming engaged with such limited fuel supplies. He handed over command to his adjutant, Captain Petrelli.

Our command tank crossed the open fields to reach the asphalt road to Damerkow. It drove carefully at first, then gradually faster. No enemy, no friend for about 2km. I had seldom seen a strip of land so dead, no shots, no sounds. This totally dead countryside seemed unnatural to me.

'This is not right! There are certainly no German troops here or we would have seen supply and rear area troops,' I dared suggest. Colonel Christern, always dashing, sometimes a little too much for my taste, waved this aside.

We drove on and on, a little faster now, but always the same scene. Suddenly I thought I saw fresh piles of earth on either side of the road well camouflaged with snow and bushes standing around that no way fitted into this winter landscape.

'Colonel, look over there with your binoculars!' 'Are you scared, Schäufler', I had become sensitive to things like this during the course of the war, but I could not say this of my commander. But I said more drastically and louder than I intended: 'God no, but I have had enough of this!' In a similar lone expedition by our colonel, we had nearly all been lost. Regimental Sergeant-Major Wegener had been killed completely unnoticed and I still had as souvenirs a splinter in my chin and a hole in my eardrum.

Colonel Christern, a tough old warrior, who was used to leading his Panzer Regiment 35 from the front and occasionally let me say something, looked at me a bit horrified. I had no time for an apology for my 'faux pas', as I spotted Soviet helmets in the thin bushes there, there and there, and the mighty barrel of a heavy anti-tank gun that was aimed at us.

'We are in the middle of the Russians!' I shouted into the ear of the nonplussed colonel. But he still doubted me, the incurable optimist. I poked the driver in the back: 'Left, a gravel pit – into it at full speed!'

The colonel shouted at me, wanting to say something but the words stuck in his throat, as the first shell whistled over our heads. The driver hit the accelerator and raced – no flew – over the snow-covered field, and braked fiercely as we slid down a steep bank of gravel just as a real fire storm broke over us.

The regimental commander, no friend of overhasty improvisations, looked at me for a short moment undecidedly. Then life returned to his face. He pointed to the radio with his chin: 'Schäufler, you see to that!'

I put on the earphones and turned the switch to 'Send' while the crew on the commander's orders took the machine gun off its mounting and climbed up the edge of the gravel pit with submachine guns and hand grenades, immediately opening fire. Each of the four men knew that the next few minutes were the most decisive in our lives and that nothing was more valuable at the moment.

'Alpenrose, Alpenrose, Alpenrose – come in urgently!' At last there was a squeak and noise in the headphones. 'Alpenrose here. What's the matter?'

'We are just short of Damerkow and surrounded by the Russians, and need help urgently. Come immediately with some tanks!'

'Alpenrose, understood. Where exactly? Three tanks are already on their way and listening in to this frequency.'

'We are in the gravel pit on the right-hand side of the road one kilometre short of the place and in a heavy fire fight. Drive along the asphalt. Give it all you've got. We will fire red Very lights.'

They were already throwing hand grenades over there. The Soviet machine guns were rattling quite near. Mortar bombs exploded in the gravel pit, showering splinters against the tank's sides.

'Alpenrose, where are you? I am firing white Very lights. Can you see them yet?'

Then we were interrupted by our Soviet listeners with diabolical laughter: 'Alpenrose, have you said your prayers yet? Now the Devil will get you!'

No, they would not get us alive, was my only thought, as this lousy lout with a Saxon accent had been tracking us since Schwetz.

I shouted to the colonel: 'Three tanks on their way. They should be here any moment!' He only raised his hand slightly and carried on firing with his submachine gun. He was already back on form.

Then, as I heard the roar of heavy engines; 'Alpenrose, fire whatever is in your barrels so that the comrades can forget us for a moment!'

High-explosive shells skimmed along the road. The fire of our crew rattled off a short burst and the Soviet fire suddenly stopped.

I threw off the headphones and crept up the side of the gravel pit. Our three tanks came racing across the snow-covered field, firing from every hatch. They charged over the anti-tank gun, crushing it into the ground. The Russians ran away in packs. They had spotted our tanks much too late to fire and aimed round at them.

I ran back to the radio set, from which the Saxon voice still came: 'Have you had enough now? Has the Devil taken you?'

For five weeks I had had to hold back from answering the lout. But now I had the greatest pleasure to give a rejoinder over the microphone.

The two radio operators and the driver returned and took their places breathing heavily, and I was able to take a look at what was taking place. The three tanks were churning around. When one has been so close to the edge of the precipice, one cannot help gloating.

The colonel came slowly up to me, smiling a bit embarrassedly, called me a stupid Bavarian and hit me on the chest, his peace offering.

We gave a short situation and location report by radio to the 4th Panzer Division, as the radio silence was already broken and they had to know that the Soviets were already in Damerkow.

In reply came an important message: 'New situation. Soviet tanks attacking Karthaus. Get ready to march immediately. Fight through to Karthaus fastest!'

Our three tanks, which had already reached the outskirts of Damerkow and were now turning around, were recalled by radio. Captain Petrelli, who had heard all the radio transmissions, reported that the train had been unloaded and all vehicles ready to move.

Karthaus? Karthaus lay 50km east of us at the entrance to Danzig. That could not be true!

After a brief issue of orders, the Christern combat group took the asphalt road east from Stolp to Danzig. At first the roads were empty of people, but soon we came upon refugee columns. The further east we went, the more there were. Suddenly we were standing opposite two wedges of humanity, a leaderless chaos. One was pressing out of Karthaus towards Stolp, the other wanted to get into the town on the same road. The refugee columns were pressing out of side streets from the south and pouring out of others from the north. In such a situation there was no going forward even for tracked vehicles. The whole of West Prussia was on the move.

One tank platoon with three vehicles was given the task of remaining to protect the refugees at the crossways near Sierke, to sort out the mess quickly, and reconnoitre a refugee route to the northeast and sign it. Nothing remained for the tanks other than to drive across country, even though that meant a greater consumption of fuel.

The regimental commander also went about this too slowly, for a catastrophe seemed to be building up in a big way in and around Karthaus. The colonel drove in with his command tank and an armoured personnel carrier platoon of Armoured Reconnaissance Battalion 4.

Arriving in Karthaus, he reported to the town commandant. This elderly colonel of the reserve, who was standing around helplessly, was completely confused and unaccustomed to such a muddled situation. Our regimental commander was subsequently appointed battle commandant of Karthaus by Corps on the afternoon of 7 March. I thus automatically had to see to the necessary radio and telephone communications for the combat area.

The first thing was to set up vehicles of Armoured Reconnaissance Battalion 4 as close security on the southern and southeastern outskirts. Chaotic circumstances reigned in the town. The streets were overfilled with refugee columns and supply vehicles, the distraught people wandering here and there with little knowledge of the threatening situation. Motor vehicles that had run out of fuel hindered the flow of traffic. There was no more going forward and no more going back. Something had to be done immediately.

Colonel Christern set all available officers and NCOs on foot rigorously directing the traffic. We established telephone communications at all crossroads, road junctions, town exits and danger points, which was possible without using too much field cable as the local telephone system was still functioning, and the exchanges were manned by soldiers.

Side roads for horse-drawn traffic were reconnoitred and signed, the columns being forced into taking them. The race for the harbours of Danzig and Gotenhafen had reached its final dramatic spurt.

One set of bad news was followed by another. Our tanks reported that they were stuck without fuel near Mooswalde, 15km from Karthaus. The other units of the 4th Panzer Division coming along with the refugee columns were making their way only quite slowly from Bütow. The leading element gave Sierakowitz as its location, about 25km west of Karthaus. Fuel delivery was hardly possible, as the blocked roads would allow no contrary traffic.

Meanwhile, troops of the Red Army had already left the German units far behind them and by the evening of 7 March were already at Seeresen, 5km southeast of Karthaus. Our armoured workshops had already moved across to Zoppot just in time.

Everyone was calling for fuel. What is the use of tanks if they are standing immobile and unable to fight on the highways! Then the owner of a civilian petrol station in Karthaus put his concealed iron tanks and also his local knowledge at our disposal. Four barrels of petrol were towed on trailers by armoured personnel carriers to Mooswalde. Naturally this was only a drop in the ocean, but perhaps it would be sufficient to reach Karthaus.

The first tank arrived at Karthaus on the morning of 8 March and was immediately sent to Seeresen, where, with the last drops of petrol, it chased the Soviets out of the place. Meanwhile, the Soviets had also taken Borkau, 6km east of Karthaus. A platoon of Armoured Reconnaissance Battalion 4 occupied Zuckau by surprise, only 20km from Danzig. The situation was more confused than ever.

A gap yawned in the front line between Seeresen and Borkau through which the Soviet armoured and infantry units marched north unhindered on 8 and 9 March. They occupied Knobelsdorf and Seefeld, and blocked the direct road to Danzig, Zoppot and Gotenhafen.

We could not prevent them, having to look on helplessly because the troops of our 4th Panzer Division and also the neighbouring divisions were tied down and hardly any of our tanks had any fuel left. Tank drivers, gunners, second-lieutenants and sergeants with Knights' Crosses ran around with canisters in their hands begging a few litres from the supply trucks to at least get their tanks into firing positions. It was enough to make one cry.

On 9 March there was unholy confusion on the roads and tracks in and around Karthaus. The anxious refugees were barely responsive. The West Prussians from the Tuchel, Konitz and Berent areas wanted to take the direct route to Danzig and could not believe that it was impossible, ignoring the alternative route via Schönwalde offered to them. The refugees from East Prussia, already six weeks on their way, and directed here, had rested in Karthaus and now pressed on, as they had once been instructed, with all their might for the roads to Pomerania, not dreaming that the Red Army had long since blocked this route. And the poorest of the poor who had fled from Pomerania, chased out by the Soviets, and who had experienced terrible things and survived, were continuing to move almost mechanically further eastwards, turning deaf ears to everything.

The local officials and Party officers, who could and should have been giving advice, were simply the first of all to leave. Without aims, leaders or plans, the streams of refugees met in Karthaus, the traffic nodal point before the gates of Danzig, mingling together in this great German upheaval.

They had been hunted by Soviet fighters. Mothers carried their dead children in their weary arms. Between the quickly snatched up belongings on the horse-drawn carts lay the torn bodies of the dead and dying next to the sick and wounded. One could see in their faces how much they had suffered on their way. They had gone on through snow and ice storms over the ice of the Frisches Haff as the Soviet artillery caused it to break up. Many, very many had died as a result of bombs and shells. The horror was in their eyes and sometimes insanity too.

And the Soviet aircraft kept on dropping millions of leaflets that rained down on the soldiers of the Red Army, and occasionally also fell on us. 'Soldiers of the Red Army – Kill the Germans! – Kill all Germans – Kill! – Kill! – Kill!' This appeal by Ilya Ehrenburg was countersigned by Joseph Stalin. As many of us had fought for three long years in Russia, mostly with a few Russian volunteers in every company, we could easily read the 'Kill! – Kill!' appeal to the Red Army soldiers.

And for weeks now we had been getting leaflets urging us to surrender. 'German soldiers! Give up your resistance! Surrender to the Red Army! We guarantee you good treatment and an immediate return home at the end of the war. If you keep on fighting, you will never see your homeland again, etc. . . . .'

How stupid did the Soviets think we were? Only very few of our division had thrown away their weapons and left women, children and comrades in the lurch. They would later regret their action for they would be subjected to the same conditions for long years in the Soviet prisoner of war camps.

That this war was lost, even the most stupid were now aware. There was absolutely nothing more to gain, no military honours, no awards, no promotions, no special leaves – only a frozen arse as the soldiers put it so strikingly every day. It was a merciless battle for naked survival for oneself and the hundred-thousand that still had faith in us wanting to get ahead of the Soviet tanks and reach Danzig or Gotenhafen, where the ships were waiting to bring them to freedom in the West.

'Kill! Kill! Kill!' The Red Army soldiers attacked us with this licence to murder in their pockets and thrust towards Danzig in a state of victorious euphoria.

To the credit of the Soviet fighting troops, it should also be said that the overwhelming majority of them were humane and behaved other than in accordance with the demands of these most inhumane of all orders in this cruel war.

Eventually on the morning of 9 March, Karthaus and the area to the north and east of it were cleared of all refugee columns and rear area transport. Only to the south and west were the convoys of trucks still jammed, the ever repeated targets of Soviet ground-attack aircraft. Corps urged and urged on the radio: 'All elements of the 4th Panzer Division are to assemble in Karthaus, on foot if necessary, with the utmost speed.' It was intended to break through on the main road to Danzig via Zuckau.

A battle group consisting of the tanks of Panzer Regiment 25 of the 7th Panzer Division, led by Major Tölke, attacked eastwards from Karthaus in two groups at 0600 hours.

One group was able to retake Knobelsdorf, and the other to shoot up five enemy tanks, but the breakthrough to Zuckau failed. The Soviets were already too strong here. Unperturbed by the German attack, they moved out of Seefeld to the north and northeast towards Kölln and Quassendorf.

Their plan was obvious. They were only marginally interested in Karthaus, wanting to cut us off here and hold us. Their target was Danzig and the acquisition of the harbours of the Danzig Bight. Although time was pressing, the assembling of the 4th Panzer Division in Karthaus was considerably delayed. After the failure of the attack, a new route was ordered along the roads Karthaus–Knobelsdorf–Wilhelmsfeld–Lebenau–Schönwalde–Steinkrug–Kollenort. The 2nd Army ordered that the high ground west of Kollenort, 20km southwest of Gotenhafen, must be held under all circumstances.

As Corps was informed, in the 4th Panzer Division the opinion was that even if the road to Zuckau was opened, the majority of the vehicles would have to be left behind for lack of fuel to take them further. In reply Corps gave the order: 'Only keep worthwhile combat vehicles. Blow up all the rest!' The outlook must be bleak.

Already on the morning of 9 March the Soviets had taken the big village of Kelpin, 6km south of Karthaus. Our own attack to close the gap in the front line between Borkau and Seeresen was only able to begin late in the afternoon because just a few of the troops of the 4th Panzer Division were able to reach the area from Karthaus. Following an announcement of the new situation and the altered withdrawal plan, it was soon called off without success. The troops of the Red Army were marching unimpeded northwards on Danzig.

The situation became more threatening by the hour. Rumours of all kinds made the murky situation even worse. It was whispered from mouth to mouth that Ivan was already in Danzig. And during the night of the 9/10 March the Soviet propaganda loudspeakers on the surrounding heights bellowed across to us: 'German soldiers! You are surrounded. You have no ammunition and no fuel any more. Surrender to the Red Army! We guarantee you . . .' The old lies. We could hardly hear them anymore. But, in view of the perilous situation, this preyed considerably on our nerves. First, we were fighting against mounting fatigue and doubt, as the Soviets countered with 'passes' and bored us with their loudspeaker appeals.

However, we waited and hoped for the promised fuel for hours and hours, and incredibly, just before the trap door finally snapped shut, all the combat vehicles that were still on the stretch west of Karthaus, were directed straight to the new route. In accordance with Corps' orders, all abandoned and inessential vehicles were tipped into the ditches and made unusable. Every litre of fuel was siphoned off beforehand and collected. Full petrol cans were found on several completely unnecessary vehicles 'for emergencies'. So something like fisticuffs reigned on the roads, idlers and dawdlers being swept aside. The tank men and grenadiers sacrificed some of their accompanying vehicles with their last items of property in order to be able to obtain a few litres of fuel.

At 0500 hours on 10 March those elements with wheeled vehicles started off on the route from Lebenau to Steinkrug, while the tanks remained in groups between Knobelsdorf and Lebenau with empty fuel tanks.

Colonel Christern, still battle commandant of Karthaus, remained with a small staff in the town, where an almost unnatural silence reigned after all the hurly-burly. The streets were as dead, swept clear. Overnight the picture had completely altered. At the town exits stood weak German security points connected to us by radio, and Soviet reconnaissance probes were repulsed with much noise. There were occasional bursts of artillery fire and attacks from Soviet aircraft. Otherwise it looked as if the enemy and friend alike had forgotten, overlooked, written us off in Karthaus.

It was reported over the radio that the divisional command post had meanwhile moved to Lensitz, 15km west of Gotenhafen. They had made it!

At 1715 hours Captain Lange reported by our radio link, which only worked part of the time, that the foremost elements of the 2nd Battalion of our Tank Regiment 35 had reached Schönwalde, but that 21 fighting vehicles had had to be left behind for lack of fuel in the vicinity of Gross-Dennemörse between Lebenau and Schönwalde.

Division radioed without comment: 'Enemy in Kölln.' Kölln lay halfway between Karthaus and Zoppot. Colonel Christern reacted in his way with: 'That's just great!'

Again there was nothing new in Karthaus on 11 March. Captain Lange, the commander of the 2nd Battalion, who had had to travel in an exposed position for his transmission to be heard, reported: 'No change in the tank situation. No fuel found. We are engaging Soviet tanks near Schönwalde.'

Another snap transmission from the 4th Panzer Division: 'Enemy tanks in Dohnasberg!' Dohnasberg lay about 6km beyond the planned assembly point near Kollenort. All the tanks of the 2nd German Army's two armoured divisions now lay immobile far from the front and scattered in groups in the woods between Karthaus and Schönwalde. This could not be good!

A small ray of light brought a communication to the battle commandant of Karthaus and Panzer Group Tölke, which was once more under command of the 4th Panzer Division. 'The fuel shortly arriving in Schönwalde is to be shared out so that at least all combat vehicles, especially tanks, armoured personnel carriers and the heavy weapons of the 4th Panzer Division and Panzer Regiment 25 get behind the new front line.'

All well and good, but Schönewalde lay 25km further north of us. We were still with the tanks of the 1st Battalion at Karthaus and Kobelsdorf, and the combat vehicles of Panzer Group Tölke were on the road to Wilhelmsfeld.

While we prepared, worried and played around, two towing vehicles came through the middle of the wood with low loaders from our tank workshops, fully laden with petrol cans. It was almost a miracle that these men had been able to find the way to us without encountering the Soviets.

To fill the tanks and send them off only took an hour. At 1700 hours they reported themselves already south of Schönwalde.

The first bad news arrived at 1900 hours. The 5th Company of Panzer Regiment 33 had been surprised and scattered by strong Soviet forces at Lebenau. They had lost all their vehicles and heavy weapons and suffered heavy casualties. And almost at the same time the 1st Battalion of the same regiment had been surrounded by enemy tanks and almost completely wiped out.

On Corps' orders, Colonel Christern left Karthaus on the night of 11/12 March under the protection of Panzer Regiment 35. We took up an all-round defensive position in Knobelsdorf.

Still on 11 March, at 2009 hours, a radio message from the 4th Panzer Division informed us: 'Fuel on the way to Schönwalde. Captain Lange there. Task after fuelling, all elements break through east to Kollenort. Own forces there!' That sounded good, but also damn bad.

At 0525 hours on 12 March the wretched fuel was at last found at the divisional command post in Lensitz, 6km east of Schönwalde.

Meanwhile, Captain Lange was engaged with the tanks of his 2nd Battalion in and around Schönwalde against Soviet tanks attacking from all sides. He held the place until the fuel vehicles arrived, the men of the 2nd Battalion holding off the angry Soviet tank attacks until the last vehicle had been refuelled, which took until noon on 13 March.

Colonel Christern had attached his small armoured group to the last tanks near Wilhelmsfeld and we met at Schönwalde during the course of the morning.

We crossed the German lines near Kollenort at 1220 hours on 13 March together with the last reconnaissance troop of Armoured Reconnaissance Battalion 4. At the same time strong Soviet tank units attacked the German positions from the northwest.

This extrication of German armoured vehicles from a hopeless situation was an exemplary display of comradely conduct by all concerned. No one felt it a sacrifice, but rather a compelling task. And already there was what binds soldiers together; the cooperation without hesitation, without pretension and without acknowledgement.

Especially outstanding were the dashing engagement of the troops of Reconnaissance Battalion 4 that stopped the Soviets near Zuckau, the brave behaviour of the 73rd Infantry Division on the positions of the heights from Dohnasberg and Quassendorf, and the repulse of all enemy attacks by the 2nd Battalion of Panzergrenadier Regiment 33 under Captain Lange, without which hardly anything would have been achieved. They had the courage to face up to the earth-shaking superpower, to draw the attention of the Soviet tanks to themselves and to hold the way free for the coming petrol-carrying vehicles and the withdrawing combat vehicles.

Nor should be forgotten the courageous commitment of both towing vehicles that brought the fuel to the tanks further south, thereby repairing some damage and saving several tanks, and bringing two of them across the lines on their low loaders.

We drove with Colonel Christern to the big, but abandoned, Adlershorst flak bunker near Zoppot and moved in for a whole night in the mighty shelter.

Much, much later we discovered that our regimental commander had had to fight bitterly for this short sleep, as we were impatiently awaited for a new commitment in Danzig-Oliva. The divisions of the Red Army were standing at the gates of Danzig.

Chapter 7

From Olivia to Heubude,
13–30 March

In mid-March the armoured divisions of the 1st Byelorussian Front under Marshal Zhukov rolled through Pomerania to the west and reached the mouth of the Oder near Stettin on 3 March.

From the south, southwest and west the 2nd Byelorussian Front under Marshal Rokossovski with five armies attacked the Danzig area from which all available shipping was ceaselessly evacuating the refugee transports over the Baltic to the West. Vast numbers of people crowded in the harbours of Danzig and Gotenhafen, driven by the hope of getting away from the threatening disaster by ship. Who wanted to remain in the country where a merciless enemy urged his soldiers forward with 'Kill Kill! Kill!' Who would voluntarily surrender themselves to the mercy of such an army!

Appointed as commander-in-chief of the German 2nd Army on 12 March, General of Armoured Troops Dietrich von Saucken, born in East Prussia and former commander of the 4th Panzer Division, sought to hold back the immense pressure of the Red Army with his exhausted divisions until all the refugees had reached safety.

With the courage of desperation the burnt-out remains of the 4th SS-Police, 7th Panzer, 215th Infantry, 32nd Infantry, 227th Infantry, 74th Infantry, 4th Panzer, 389th Infantry, 252nd Infantry, 12th Luftwaffe Field, 542nd Volksgrenadier, 337th Infantry, 35th Infantry, 83rd Infantry and 23rd Infantry Divisions braced themselves in a wide curve around Gotenhafen and Danzig against the enemy, while the 7th Infantry Division still held out between the Vistula and the Frisches Haff lagoon.

The heavy cruiser *Prinz Eugen,* the old battleship *Schlesien* and the light cruiser *Leipzig* supported the heavily pressed front from the sea with their limited ammunition holdings. The salvoes from the heavy naval guns howled over Danzig and hit the thick ranks of the attacking Soviets with astounding accuracy, bringing temporary relief.

In the Gluckau area, about 6km southwest of Danzig-Oliva, on 14 March, Colonel Christern's armoured combat group of the 4th Panzer Division prepared to attack in order to close a gap in the front between Pempau and Zuckau which had opened up at this time. We were to come in here from the east exactly where we had been unable to from the west five days earlier.

For this attack on 15 March we had been promised further fire support from the ships' artillery, as the division's own Armoured Artillery Regiment 103 had hardly any ammunition left. A naval fire direction officer had already reported to Colonel Christern. The dark silhouettes of the warships could be seen out there in the Danzig Bight. A permanently sited naval coastal battery would join in as far as its guns could swing round, and a heavy flak battery from the Danzig air defences would also be available.

But the situation changed. The Soviets attacked our Panzer Regiment 12's sector with two to three divisions. In bitter defensive fighting the positions could only be held with the above-named fire support. Second-Lieutenant Graf Moltke alone shot up six Soviet tanks near Pempau. The weather was clear and the Soviets were able to deploy their aircraft constantly, against which we had absolutely nothing to engage them with. The German Luftwaffe was no longer available. The flak was engaged in the ground fighting role and was forbidden to expend its valuable ammunition against aircraft.

On the other hand the troops of the Red Army had ammunition in abundance, and were not sparing it. They unloaded it practically before our eyes at Zuckau railway station, as they knew that we were unable to disturb them. Russian specialist troops had got the German railway system working up to here astoundingly quickly.

Again and again the Soviets ran up to our lines of Panzergrenadiers. However, we were able to prevent a breakthrough here. Afterwards they switched their attacks further north to our neighbouring division.

This was the situation when on 15 March Lieutenant Gerlach of Panzer Regiment 35 was ordered by Colonel Christen to drive to the Raumkau-Neue Welt area with those Panthers available to support the 389th Infantry Division, located there against impending Soviet tank attacks.

Robert Poensgen, a war correspondent with the 4th Panzer Division, described the event:

Shortly before setting off one of the *Panthers* had to be detached to one of the regiment's other combat teams in whose sector heavy Soviet tanks of the *Joseph Stalin* type had been reported. During the move two *Panthers* fell out because of too much water in their petrol tanks. Just before nightfall Lieutenant Gerlach reached the engagement area and received the order to accompany a fusilier battalion's night attack on the village of Neue Welt and, after destroying the reported enemy tanks, to block the gap between the lakes.

The fusiliers attacked at about 2000 hours. It was already pitch dark. The attack came up against heavy fire. One could clearly hear the firing of many tanks.

Meanwhile it had been realised that there were no less than 24 enemy tanks, including 8 *Joseph Stalin* tanks in Neue Welt, and Gerlach was expected to engage these earth-shaking monsters in their lairs with only two *Panthers*! He sought every way of getting out of this unequal situation, which would most likely have to end to the advantage of the Soviets. But the attack on the village had to be pursued at whatever the cost.

'Make your wills, comrades!' was the only advice that Gerlach could give this men, and he was certainly no pessimist or irresolute person, having already led about 150 tank attacks, but this seemed to him to be a suicide mission. Certainly there were no novices in either of the *Panthers,* but battle-proven tank men who had long since made up their minds and were prepared to follow the path of duty to the bitter end.

As the fusiliers of the 389th Infantry Division reached the village, they knocked out an enemy tank and an anti-tank gun with panzerfausts, but then came under fierce fire that pushed them back a bit. At this inopportune moment Lieutenant Gerlach's command tank broke down. The tank had been badly over-strained during the last weeks and not received sufficient maintenance. He had to send the tank and its crew back so as not to lose it forever. He climbed into the last tank with his trusty radio operator, Sergeant Kupfer, who being a young inexperienced soldier sat at the set. Now only old hands were in their fighting positions: gun-aimer Sergeant Lang, gun-loader Lance-Corporal Heinrich and driver, Senior Corporal Bauer.

All alone, the *Panther* crept along the railway line into the village, the engine running softly in order not to betray itself through the noise.

As an old experienced tank man, Gerlach knew well that he would have to make an exceptional start if he was to come out of this unequal fight. He was shielded from enemy view by a snow fence and standing on the railway track beside him were goods wagons, so the tank's outline would not show against the horizon when it became light.

They were about 400 metres from the village when the *Panther* hit a soft patch. It took all the driver's skill to get it going again. As a result of the unavoidable increase in engine noise, the Soviets were alerted and fired blindly in the suspected direction, but without seeing or even hitting the well-hidden tank.

The gun-aimer, Lang, fired at the gun flashes and with his first shot hit a self-propelled gun, which burst into flames together with the barn behind it, lighting up the surrounding area. Two further Soviet tanks guarding the village perimeter were identified near the barn.

Now that the *Panther* came under increased and above all aimed fire, Gerlach drove down the reverse slope until he could observe the enemy-occupied village through his periscope. Enemy tanks were standing around between the buildings in thick clumps. Strong artillery and mortar fire commenced, the enemy having no need to conserve ammunition.

At about midday on the 16th March another *Panther* commanded by Sergeant-Major Palm, the 'Tank Cracker', arrived in support. During the course of the afternoon this tank set on fire another two enemy tanks, including a *Joseph Stalin*. Gerlach was able to put another *Joseph Stalin* out of action and to destroy a heavy assault gun. Several anti-tank guns were also destroyed.

Thus passed the remainder of the day and the night leading to the 17th March, the Soviets not daring to emerge from cover. Only at daybreak did they try an attack again on the right with infantry support. Gerlach immediately drove to the threatened site.

Whilst he himself was engaging the enemy tanks as they appeared, his radio NCO used machine-gun fire to keep the Soviet infantry at bay.

The two German *Panthers* not only drove back a company of Russian infantry in this fight, from good positions they shot up a further five *Joseph Stalins,* another heavy Soviet tank, three assault guns and a heavy anti-tank gun.

Gerlach was also engaged with his two tanks on the following day, the 18th March, in the same sector with the 389th Infantry Division. From a very favourable height in a bitter fire duel, another *Joseph Stalin,* two assault guns and two anti-tank guns were destroyed and three further enemy tanks set on fire.

How severe the bodily stress and demands in this kind of day and night battle of life and death are, is best shown by the circumstances in which Lieutenant Gerlach abruptly fell asleep during the course of a conversation with the infantry regimental command post.

The result of these three days of fighting was 21 heavy and ultra heavy enemy tanks destroyed without any loss on our side.

It was not just the clever conduct of the engagement, the friction-free cooperation of the old tank hands, but predominently the iron will of the ten men behind the steel plating to keep the way to life free for the women and children and their wounded comrades.

The mass of the 4th Panzer Division was still engaged in heavy defensive fighting between Ramkau and Zuckau, about 16km west of Danzig, our tanks supporting the grenadiers to good effect.

At 0900 hours on 16 March the Soviets attacked with two infantry divisions and tanks. Second-Lieutenant Graf Moltke repulsed all enemy attacks with his small group of tanks until 1700 hours, shooting up nine Soviet tanks. Three further tanks were destroyed with panzerfausts, two of them by Senior Corporal Schöbel of the 5th Company, Panzergrenadier Regiment 12.

Losses on both sides were very high. The panzergrenadier casualties were made up with fresh supply troops found in Danzig city, where they were rounded up by the military police in a 'Heroes' Roundup' operation.

There was a host of administrative postions that long had had nothing to do, supply regiments eking out an existence, although all supply routes had long since been interrupted. There were staffs that had long since lost their troops. In short, Danzig was overfull of soldiers of the rear services that had become redundant. They were now extracted as replacements for the casualties among the fighting troops. Every day the Panzergrenadiers received a large number of these men unused to combat.

The troops' opinion of this action was: 'By the time one had taken their names, some were already wounded or had vanished. An elderly senior corporal with two or three men held as much of a section of the front as twenty or thirty of these combed out, untrained people lacking front-line experience.'

One day Panzergrenadier Regiment 12 was also allocated a tank-destroyer company of 14 Danzig Hitler Youth, about 15 years old and equipped with bicycles and panzerfausts. These youngsters behaved like grown-ups and were convinced of the importance of their task. There was an unusual earnestness in their childish faces. The grenadiers looked after them, discreetly took their panzerfausts off them and let them have a long sleep in their positions before sending the youngsters off home to their mothers, where they belonged.

Our Armoured Artillery Regiment 103 operated with the few shells available to it against enemy assembly areas in Zuckau and its railway station. Army Anti-Aircraft Battalion 290 received permission to engage the carelessly low-flying Soviet aircraft and shot down seventy-five of them.

On the 16th March the village of Ramkau was lost, although the main front line held.

The removal of refugees and wounded by sea from Gotenhafen and Danzig was continuing at top speed, although the ships' berths were under constant Soviet air attack.

On 17 March the High Command announced that the commander of the 4th Panzer Division, General Clemens Betzel, had been awarded the Oak Leaves to his Knight's Cross. In the division's daily orders, the general thanked his soldiers for their exemplary bravery that had qualified him for this high award.

Indicative of the everyday hectic activity was the reprimand from the Corps' chief-of-staff on 18 March as the mass of Panzergrenadier Regiment 33 and part of Panzer Regiment 35 were transferred to the 252nd Infantry Division, and the *Panthers* of Panzer Regiment 35 were still successfully fighting in the 389th Infantry Division's sector: 'The commanding general is disappointed that the 389th Infantry Division can hold against an enemy with 30 tanks, but the 4th Panzer Division is not in a position to hold Height 164.9.'

General Betzel reported simply: 'The battalions and the majority of this division are engaged with the neighbouring division. Only two tanks are operational. The divisional artillery, despite their ammunition state, have behaved excellently. Without troops it was impossible to take Height 164.9 by assault.'

On the night leading to 19 March the refugee-overfilled city of Danzig was hit by a devastating bombing attack from 300 to 400 American *Superfortresses* coming from the west and flying off eastwards. We had to watch this sad dance of death from our positions on the heights west of the town without doing anything, not a bomb falling on the fighting troops. On the night of the 20th they came back from the east, dropped their bomb loads on the city virtually unhindered and flew off to the west. The city's meagre air defences could do little against them.

Soviet aircraft were in the air all day long without a break. The fighters with the red stars on their wings fired with their weapons on every individual vehicle on the roads, and blasted the forward lines with their rockets. The population of Danzig could only leave their shelter of their cellars for a few minutes at a time.

On 20 March, following a bombardment of several hours between Bastenhagen and Leeson, the Soviets attacked along the whole divisional front with three fresh rifle divisions and thirty tanks. These attacks were also continued with undiminished intensity on 21 March. The Soviets had long since noticed our lack of ammunition and often moved up quite close behind the forward lines, bringing their supplies directly up to the attacking troops.

The lack of ammunition and fuel for the German troops was only partly a real shortcoming. Certainly the depots had been instructed to eke out their issues as it was uncertain whether further deliveries could be expected from bombed-out central Germany. Apart from this, every journey to the troops with the highly explosive loads was a 'suicide mission' with Soviet air superiority, and the strict traffic controls, necessary in this situation, delayed the deliveries and made them more difficult.

There were ever more small breaches in the German lines, but the enemy aim of breaking through to Danzig could still be denied by the brave defence put up by the troops.

It was also possible to hold back the Red Army divisions some distance from the Baltic Sea, thus keeping the still continuing refugee movements and large concentrations of people out of the range of the Soviet artillery.

This desperate defensive battle on the high ground west of Danzig against a superior enemy attacking again and again with heavy weapons, tanks and ammunition in abundance, his numerical and materiel advantage utilised to the utmost, brought a high blood count on the German side. Many of the combatant companies had shrunk down to ten to twenty men, the panzergrenadier battalions mostly to company strength. The reinforcements delivered by Operation 'Heroes' Roundup' could not make up for these losses.

On the other hand, the quartermaster staff, workshop and supply personnel of our own division were in danger of being grabbed, taken in and allocated to a completely strange infantry unit or emergency company by the military police commandos.

Armoured Artillery Regiment 103 formed an 'Artillery Company' from those gunners that had lost their guns and attached it to Panzergrenadier Regiment 12 in the infantry role. This way the men remained within the divisional framework in comradely units and fought under the command of officers and NCOs that they trusted.

The tank crews without tanks in our Panzer Regiment 35 were formed into a tank-destroyer company, armed with machine guns, submachine guns, pistols and panzerfausts. These men were commanded by Second-Lieutenant Klaus Schiller, who had lost an arm in an earlier wounding but nevertheless volunteered to return to the front line.

On 21 March the Soviets launched their attack on the whole of the Danzig western front and were able to thrust through to the Danzig Bight, north of Zoppot. The naval ships effectively supported the German troops' defensive fighting, but were unable to prevent the Soviets occupying the famous Baltic bathing resort of Zoppot. The Danzig bridgehead was now divided into three parts: the Hela peninsula, the naval harbour of Gotenhafen with Oxhöft, and the bigger bridgehead with Danzig harbour that included the mouths of the Vistula and the Frische Nehrung spit.

The Soviets occupying the high ground west of Oliva now had a direct view of the city of Danzig lying below. They used this enormous advantage, quickly building up their artillery positions for their death thrust on Danzig.

One did not have to wait long. On 23 March a hurricane of fire of unparalleled proportions fell on the Danzig suburbs. The term 'barrage' does not suffice for this. This was a unique, gigantic primeval scream, an ear deafening din of battle without pause, an hour-long lasting succession of explosions from shells, rockets and mortars. All telephone communications were permanently destroyed and no telephone apparatus forward of the regimental command posts remained operational, so they continued to be uncertain of the situation at the front line for a long time. Only those that had tanks nearby could report over their short-wave radios.

Following this fearsome barrage, the Soviet divisions launched their main attack at 1120 hours, their aim being Burgraben, about 10km west of Danzig.

The hard-tested 2nd Battalion of Panzer Regiment 33, which was now only of company strength, both the self-propelled gun batteries of Armoured Artillery Regiment 103, the 'Artillery Company' and the tank-destroyer company of our Panzer Regiment 35 were sent to Nenkau. Once the Soviet attack had been dealt with, a new line of defence was to be established along the line of the heights from Martern via Klein Kelpin to Nenkau.

Klaus Schiller, the one-armed Second-Lieutenant and commander of the tank-destroyer company, described his experience here in writing:

It was the end of March 1945. Nobody knew exactly what day of the week it was, or the date. We had lost all sense of time and the interest in it in the furnace of Danzig. The rumour that we would be shipped back home to a new unit suddenly fell silent. Instead we were issued with panzerfausts, machine guns, submachine guns and hand grenades. This certainly did not look as if the remaining crews of shot-up tanks were about to be issued with new ones.

We played cards, wrote letters, which – perhaps – would reach home, to cover the agonising uncertainty. We took this short rest, the switching off of combat alertness, as essential, perhaps the final preparation for something awaiting us with eerie inevitability.

We could still hear the thunder of the front line in the distance. We had long become accustomed to the howling of the sirens, the bellowing of the flak, the falling of the bombs, to these cruel, regular sounds of battle that provided the background to the destruction of the lovely inner city of Danzig.

All these men were aware that Danzig was one big mousetrap. Then an order from regiment stiffened us like a whistle blast: 'A tank-destroyer company will be formed from the remains of shot-up tank companies. It will destroy tanks in close-quarter fighting under the protection of the infantry and so check the enemy advance. The positions are to be occupied by 1500 hours. Contact will be established with the infantry units.'

Platoons and sections were quickly divided up so that the ties of old comradeship were not lost. Trucks took us close to the allocated positions. Despite everything, we sang the songs that we had always sung.

Before dusk we sought the prepared trenches right and left of the road to Danzig. In front of us was the village of Nenkau with a hill before it. The company was split into two platoons led by experienced NCOs. After a final briefing, we split up. The goodbyes had a special resonance on this occasion, at least to me. The farewell handshake lasted a second longer than usual.

We knew from previous engagements that we could be abandoned unconditionally in extreme situations, even if for weeks the motto 'save yourself, if you can' had been circulating unspoken through the city.

Figures, singly and in groups, hastened towards us through the darkness heading for Danzig. To our questions they answered distraughtly: 'Ivan is attacking!' To improve our knowledge of the situation, I stamped through the mud with a few comrades to the dark groups of buildings. The warm felt boots sometimes stood up by themselves. There we met our own infantrymen with whom we had already made contact that afternoon. Instead of lying down behind machine guns, they were calmly smoking their pipes, so it could not be so bad. They belonged to the unit positioned on the hill in front of the village.

We described our exact position to them again and promised not to let them down if there was a tank attack. Reassured, we returned to our trenches. The village lay under artillery and mortar fire.

Towards midnight Russian voices came closer. In the pauses between the firing we could clearly hear them urging their horses forward with 'Davei'. The purring of heavy engines was well known to us and the iron clanking of tank tracks we had already heard for a considerable time. It must be the sound of a T-34 coming towards us. Then the tank tracks made a harder clang on the village street. The first tanks must soon appear near the buildings.

The skies were lightened by the flash of guns and explosions and from individual fires. We stalked in pairs in the shadows of trees and buildings. Our machine-gun team was to give us covering fire should Soviet infantry be escorting the tanks.

We head the clattering and short squeak of the tank tracks nearby. We could clearly make out a T-34 on the roadside with its gun threateningly seeking a target over us, so the steel colossus was at its least dangerous. Despite the sharpest observation, we could see no Soviet infantry. So, let's go!

We carefully made our way closer to the steel monster; 50 metres, 40, 30, and there was a shell hole. The fire trail from our panzerfaust ripped through the darkness – two seconds in which our hearts stood still – and then a bright flash and a loud bang – direct hit!

Some screams, a turret flew open and shocked figures fell out and vanished crouched over into the night. We did not open fire. The tank caught fire and began to burn with loud explosions.

This spontaneous greeting appeared to impress the Soviets, who broke off their night attack, leaving their guns and mortars to speak for them. Suddenly an anxious silence reigned.

With the dawn we discovered the reason for this unusual lack of noise. The exhausted, decimated infantry had abandoned the hill in front of the village and not told us of their withdrawal. That was not nice, but who can hold it against the fatigue of the half-dead infantrymen?

What should we do now? If we cleared, the small bridgehead, our 1st Platoon and the Bavarian infantry unit with it would be cut off. An occupation of the abandoned position in front of the village by our black-uniformed men with only limited trench and close-quarter fighting experience would be a risky business. But we had had to see so much in the foregoing weeks: refugee treks with fleeing families being driven ahead of them by the Soviet tanks and those on the way to the coast mercilessly shot up when they did not go fast enough. Should we betray these poor victims of war that placed their hopes in us? Their thanks made the decision a light one.

We made our way forward individually into the Soviet artillery fire. We had already lost two killed. Then we occupied the abandoned position on the hill. Nevertheless, we could only hold this advance bastion for a few hours, while the Soviets considerably underestimated our strength. Only when we realised that there were no German troops to our right and left, did we withdraw slowly from the enemy at about midday and assembled at the village exit. We were worried about our 1st Platoon, not having had any contact since dawn.

It was only much later that we learnt that, despite our

counterattack, which we had undertaken on its behalf, it had been surrounded by the Soviets and almost completely wiped out. Only very few had come through unscathed.

We ourselves were pushed back into the witches' cauldron of Danzig by the Soviets attacking from all sides. All those still alive and unwilling to surrender to the Soviets without a fight, were lying behind barricades, the remains of walls, kerbstones and even gravestones. We could hear the calls of the weary and tired coming from the cellars: 'Throw your weapons away!' These despairing voices were not threatening, they were begging.

There were also soldiers among them that thought they could be spared if they covered themselves with a bit of civilian clothing. Even some of our men were unable to resist this temptation. One despatch rider vanished without trace. Another soldier urgently asked me to allow him to break through to the battalion behind as he had a wife and children at home. I could not resist his appeal and wrote out a message about our action until now to the 1st Battalion, as without a duty assignment the man would be picked up by the military police and handed over to the standing court martial.

One should not condemn too quickly. Every one of us was wrestling with the answer to the question: fight on or give up? Should we listen to those lacking courage in the cellars, or should we help the tens of thousands on the beaches by holding on?

In no case would we want to be shamed in front of our comrades one day. That is why we continued with the battle for Danzig, even if we decided to do so quite alone.

During the last days of the street fighting we had developed a successful tank-destroying tactic. We went through the attics, which were connected as an air raid precaution, using them as cover to get to the leading Soviet tanks. We put one man with a submachine gun at the window to cover us, and aimed our panzerfausts through holes in the roofs at the enemy tanks. The effect on the Soviets was quite devastating when suddenly a T-34 flew into the air. We used the confusion among the enemy to get away undetected and seek another target. In this manner we forced the Soviets to advance quite slowly and cautiously. Every hour, every fought-out day was so tremendously important for the refugees. There was no lack of panzerfausts, they were lying about everywhere. Unfortunately the food supplies were not so good.

We had some dead and wounded in an engagement from behind a street barricade. Over their graves we promised never to forget them. We prayed God to look after their families and to give us strength in this merciless fight. We could feel how self-doubt and the hell around us were threatening to suffocate us.

Only when the centre of Danzig was in flames and the bridges collapsing did we withdraw over the arm of the Vistula one by one into the suburb of Heubude. I saw the famous Crane Tower for the first and last time in my life from a burning, slowly collapsing bridge as it burst into flames. I was overtaken by a deep depression, and yet every life saved was worth a thousand times more than all these historic buildings together. I was talking to myself confusedly. A bitter laughing scared me. As I stumbled on I realised that it was my own laughter.

I met up with all the comrades that had withstood the hell of Danzig alive and were one way or another intact once more in Heubude. I felt deeply gratified, for the comradeship in war was really something quite unique.

Although the evacuation of Danzig had commenced on 20 March, the shocked inhabitants no longer dared to go on the streets, which lay under fire from low-flying aircraft. The fear of an uncertain future in this obscure situation also paralysed their ability to decide. The fate of the *Wilhelm Gustloff* and the *General Steuben* had circulated so that many refugees waiting for ships on the quay had sought shelter in the city's air raid shelters as the exploding shells grew ever nearer and the air attacks increased. However, the majority had sought shelter in the wooded dunes near Heubude and Krakau, as a small vessel had started a shuttle service from Neufáhr to Hela.

Until now the American night bombers in their west–east, east–west flights had principally targeted the centre of Danzig, but on the night of 22/23 March they made a big attack on Heubude, Krakau and Neufáhr, killing thousands of women and children as there were no air raid shelters.

The Soviets opened their bombing attack over the centre of Danzig on 24 March. Rockets hissed from the wings of the IL-2s. Fires flared up everywhere and grew into epidemic proportions. Despite all the efforts, they could not be contained because the city's power and water supplies had been destroyed during the night.

The asphalt layers on the streets and bridges caught fire and clouds of smoke darkened the skies, making breathing difficult, particularly in the cellars. Many people died in the shelters. The sirens screamed even more frightfully. There were no fighters on our side, and hardly any anti-aircraft gunfire. A few aircraft tumbled away after being hit by machine-gun fire, but the apocalyptic mood in the dying city just increased.

Once the general confusion had reached its climax, the bombers came back again, but now they were dropping leaflets, millions of them dancing slowly out of the smoke-laden sky. Marshal Rokossovsky hoped to weaken our resolve. The complete wording of his leaflet is worth repeating:

APPEAL BY MARSHAL ROKOSSOVSKY
TO THE GARRISONS OF DANZIG AND GDINGEN!

Generals, officers and soldiers of the 2nd German Army!
My troops took Zoppot yesterday, the 23rd March, and split the surrounding groups of forces into two parts. The garrisons of Danzig and Gotenhafen have been separated from one another. Our artillery is firing on the harbours of Danzig and Gotenhafen and the approaches to them. The iron ring of my troops is closing in on your troops even more.

Under these conditions, your resistance is senseless and will only lead to your destruction as well as that of hundreds of thousands of women, children and the elderly.

I demand that you:
1. Immediately abandon your resistance and surrender with white flags individually, in groups, by platoons, companies, battalions or regiments.

2. All that surrender I guarantee their lives and the retention of their personal effects. All officers and soldiers that do not throw down their arms will be destroyed in the impending storm.

You will be fully responsible for the sacrifice of the civilian population.

The 24th March 1944 The Commander
of the troops of the 2nd Byelorussian Front
Marshal of the Soviet Union
Rokossovsky

This appeal was sent in writing, but only very few trusted the word of the Soviet marshal. Certainly, the battle in Danzig was hopeless from a military point of view. With a fair opponent, this appeal made sense, but not with the one here that had given free licence to his troops to murder, rape and plunder. The few trusting and weak souls that surrendered to the Red Army had a years-long opportunity to think about it in Soviet prisoner of war camps. 'Retention of personal possessions', 'good handling' and 'immediate repatriation after the war', as the Soviet propaganda loudspeakers had been bawling out for weeks, were all absolute lies.

Consequently, the Soviet marshal's appeal achieved no sweeping success. The German soldiers were unwilling to abandon the civilian population to the capriciousness of the Red Army, to hand them over for massacre as at Nemmersdorf.

Marshal Rokossovsky answered the German soldiers' refusal the following day, 25 March, Palm Sunday, with a vehement air attack on the centre of Danzig. Almost all the old historic buildings there were destroyed. Even the venerable old Marienkirche was hit. The sea of flames reached undreamt of proportions. The constant artillery fire forced the people into the cellars, where many suffocated. The last ship lying in Danzig's Neufahrwasser harbour, the large 9,555-ton *Ubena*, took on the last of the refugees sheltering there while under artillery fire. Shortly after her departure, the two German ammunition ships, the *Bille* and the *Weser,* blew up.

We were lying in foxholes quite close to the enemy on a steep hill, which was also known as the Zigankenberg, as the Danzig suburbs below us shook from the continuous shelling and explosions from aerial bombardment. Captain Kahle, the new regimental adjutant, and Captain Schalmat, the workshop commander and an always cheerful East Prussian, were killed on that day.

Second-Lieutenant Graf Rüdiger von Moltke, as his full title went, although little known in our Panzer Regiment 35, where he went by his rank or as 'the boss' and by his friends as 'Molch', stood with his tank platoon a few hundred metres in front of us and did not let the Soviets get one step closer.

The order had come from Division to dissolve our regimental headquarters staff and send all combat ready vehicles to the 1st Battalion. Captain Kästner was to command them as before. The released staff had to be given to Panzergrenadier Regiment 12 as infantrymen, a hard lot for these experienced tank men. Their only consolation was that they remained together and within the 4th Panzer Division.

Our former regimental commander, Colonel Christern, had to take over the command of the 7th Panzer Division, which was fighting in the separate bridgehead of Gotenhafen. General Mauss had been severely wounded and had to leave his division. The colonel bade a hearty farewell to the men in his immediate vicinity. He gave me the choice of either going to Gotenhafen with him as his liaison officer, or to the 1st Battalion as Signals Officer. I was undecided at first, but then quickly decided to remain with my comrades in Danzig.

'But come with me part of the way,' he asked. I could do that. I could not very well refuse my regimental commander with whom I had shared so many experiences, and had so many scrapes, although, quite honestly, I had no desire to drive to Neufahr through the hail of Soviet shells on Danzig.

He climbed into his command vehicle for the last time. The radio remained switched off, and that was new, but with whom should we be in contact now? Panzer Regiment 35 had ceased to exist some hours ago.

Masses of rubble lay on the streets and there were fires all around us. The city was almost empty of people. Through the clouds of smoke in front of us appeared the facade of a church, almost undamaged. The colonel wanted to stop here. He climbed out and asked the driver and myself to accompany him.

In the semi darkness we entered the nave of the church, which had suffered little from the war. The colonel looked searchingly around, then a small smile lit up his battle-weary face. He silently indicated that I should sit down on a bench. He and the driver then went up some steep steps. I sat somewhat uncomfortably on the heavy wooden bench, hearing the sounds of war coming from outside. I was suddenly startled. A quite strange sound reached me through my battle-damaged ear – the organ roared out, overcoming the murdering sounds, soon enabling me to forget the war around. A unique, nostalgic feeling overcame me, and the gloomy church suddenly seemed so light.

Of course, I knew that the colonel was very fond of music and played several instruments, but now I was listening to him playing an organ for the first time, and he was playing brilliantly, taking me away from the sounds of war to memories of carefree peacetime days. All the misery in me vanished: war and destruction, death and horror. The wonderful sounds of the cheerful melodies enabled me to believe in a future once more.

But could there be another morning for us, dammed by war? Would we ever experience a time in which we would not have to kill in order not to be killed ourselves? These were questions for which no short answer sufficed.

I still do not know today how long I had listened and dreamt when the colonel clapped me on the shoulder, bringing me back to reality. His face was as if enlightened.

We climbed into the APC without saying a word. Gradually, the sounds of the fighting came back to me. At Neufähr harbour the colonel said a brief farewell, walked off quickly and climbed into the motor boat waiting for him. He waved back at me, and I forgot to salute him properly. He looked thoughtfully straight ahead, already thinking about his new task.

The sounds of the organ still rang in me as I drove back through the burning city to Zigankenberg, where the battle for Danzig was raging.

And then everything went blow by blow. The last tanks were fighting between Schidlitz and Emaus, covering towards the south, while the Soviets came ever nearer from the direction of Nenkau. The 1st Battalion commanded by Captain Kästner had taken over the former regimental command post in Zigankenberg and we were lying in foxholes in the steep eastern cliffs. From there we had a gruesome round view at our feet of the city of Danzig being systematically shot to pieces by the Red Army's guns. Poisonous yellow clouds of smoke arose from the ruins, quickly becoming darker in colour. Brilliant fires blazed in the streets and grew hour by hour into a sea of fire.

The Soviets had reached the heights west of Danzig on 25 March. The lower ground in which the city was spread out was like a gift for them. From above they could observe every movement and bring it under fire.

Ever new Soviet bombers roared over us, dropping their bombs. Fighters swept over us with nerve-shattering attacks, firing their rockets and returning to rake with their machine guns those positions that had dared to fire on them with hand-held weapons.

From Bohnsack and Neufähr engineer ferries ran a shuttle service taking the last of the refugees to Hela. The people crowded on the Vistula that had suffered severely under the Soviet air attacks grew less from hour to hour. Some of them wanted to go on further towards Schiewenhorst. Anyhow, it could now be seen when the last civilian had left the inferno of Danzig.

Telephone communications were hardly reparable. Messages and orders forward of the divisional command post were mainly conveyed via the tanks' UVF radios, the radios of the non-armoured troops having either been shot up or become unserviceable. All the units of the 389th and 252nd Infantry Divisions and the 12th Luftwaffe Field Division fighting in the city, now known as 'combat teams' because of their diminished strengths, voluntarily subordinated themselves to the command of the 4th Panzer Division, as communications with Corps and Army were permanently interrupted.

On 26 March the health resort of Oliva was lost after a hard struggle. During the following night the district of Langfuhr was abandoned without a fight as the evacuation of refugees from Danzig was virtually complete. Details were no longer recorded by the overwhelmed authorities. The mass of those involved had long crossed over. Only when it was possible to switch off completely would it be feasible to absorb what was going on.

General Betzel, the commander of the 4th Panzer Division, who was conducting the construction of a defensive belt at the Oliva Gate on the afternoon of 27 March, was so badly wounded by a Soviet bombardment that he died on the spot. Major Knoche, the commander of Panzergrenadier Regiment 33, was also severely wounded and had to give up his command.

Although the news of the death of their much-loved and respected divisional commander in this precarious situation was held back at first, it spread like wild fire from company to company and put a further strain on the bravely fighting men.

The command of the 4th Panzer Division was taken over on the 2nd Army's orders by the esteemed commander of Panzergrenadier Regiment 12, Colonel Hoffmann, a typical front-line officer, an adventurous man and a tank man since the very first. He had belonged to the tank troops since 1935 and to the 4th Panzer Division since its formation in 1938. He had gone from command of the 1st Company to being commander of Panzergrenadier Regiment 12. He was the second soldier in the division to be awarded the Knights' Cross and had been awarded the Oak Leaves to it for the breakout from Kovel. So our 4th Panzer Division remained in good hands.

Colonel Hoffmann had taken over command of the division not only at the worst time, but had also undertaken the quite insoluble task of getting it out of this precarious situation and leading it through the last stage of the war.

On the night of 27/28 March the German troops withdrew eastwards behind the Mottlau River, abandoning the western part of the city. As the soldiers prepared to withdraw, many inhabitants of Danzig city decided to join them who previously had not been prepared to give up their homes, and belongings. This brought problems along with it.

The withdrawal from the burning, dying city was a sad sight. With the retreating troops went the dead General Betzel on his command tank, covered with a Reichs War Flag.

Otto Alexander von Müller, then lieutenant and liaison officer on the staff of the 4th Panzer Division, formulated his thoughts on the withdrawal from Danzig:

27th March 1945
Dead General! Instead of a bier,
Your tank carries you. Instead of a coffin,
A blood-stained greatcoat covers you.
Instead of a flaming torch,
Fires blaze over you
The plaintive cry groans
With the death wound of the dying city.

You yourself were the last
To throw yourself before its gate. Shattered, we formed the
rearguard, Taking you with us
And fought deadly pale
In your stead.

Dead General!
The hard tank tracks grind Smoking scars in the fallen
ashes. White-glowing ruins collapse, Showering down.
Chaos thunders Around a cramped existence.

The dead shudders –
Is he writhing?
No, only the tank bumps
Over black lumps.
Is he crying out?
No – only the engine is howling
Under its bitter load.

Dead General!
Fallen, we follow you
Out of this lost city and battle.

There was still fighting in the eastern part of Danzig city on 29 March, the last rearguards disengaging from the enemy that night.

Late on the afternoon of the 29th I received the order to drive to the battalion's new command post alongside the Vistula with my radio crew in an armoured personnel carrier. The adjutant, Lieutenant Grigat, should already be there, so I was told.

The tracks churned laboriously over debris covering the roadway. I recalled the distance to Heubude by road being about 3km. I had selected the shortest route to the Vistula Bridge precisely from the map, as we wanted to leave the city, which lay under heavy fire, quickly and without difficulty. But the destruction around us was so great that it was difficult to find one's way in this confusion. Here and there we came across little groups of distraught soldiers that had lost their way.

After a back-breaking journey over chunks of wall, concrete blocks, past falling gables, through air attacks, Stalin-Organ salvoes and constant artillery fire, we reached the end of a long queue of vehicles.

We waited for a while with the usual patience that soldiers are accustomed to in war. But the delay here was uncomfortable. Somewhere an anti-tank gun was firing at regular intervals. Around us vehicles of all kinds were burning, ammunition exploding, splinters flying. But no one near and far appeared to be bothered. That made me thoughtful. This prompted me to going to the head of this column. This was risky and very arduous, but was worth it in the end.

Looking back, I could see that almost all the vehicles were unoccupied. The men had apparently continued on foot, abandoning their vehicles in the middle of the road to the annoyance of those following.

I further discovered that there was now only a distance of about 300m to the Vistula Bridge. A second glance revealed that these 300 metres were inconceivably horrible with bloated horse carcases, burnt-out trucks, metre-deep bomb craters, dead, dead, dead – burnt and torn apart. And among the smoking vehicles some distraught drivers sat at the steering wheels, staring at the truck in front, waiting for it to move on, but the men sitting at the steering wheels were dead.

This shook me. Get away from here! We climbed in our cross-country half-track over mounds of debris, drove through gardens and backyards, and reached the bridge just at the moment when a strong group of Soviet bombers approached it. What should we do?

Bombs could fall everywhere, and we were already dulled by all kinds of dangers. The main thing was that the bridge was still there. Nobody could say how much longer this only remaining whole crossing over the Vistula would be usable. So we raced forward, as it was wonderfully empty at this point, and that was lucky for us.

We tumbled into shell holes, crunched over bits of concrete, bombs hissing left and right, shaking our vehicle about as they exploded with an ear-shattering din in the river bed, and splinters clattered against the vehicle sides. Fountains of water rose into the sky, showering us. It was a journey into Hell. I stared determinedly through the observation slit, forced to see how the bridge was being torn by a bomb blast on one side, how it swayed but held.

Everyone around was lying under cover, pressing their noses flat in the dirt, only we, quite alone, rattled and bumped along, observing anxiously the open bomb doors above us, and breathed out again as we sensed the firm ground under our tracks.

And over there on the other bank were again burning vehicles, the cadavers of horses, destroyed military equipment, the debris of war stacked up as far as the eye could see, burying the dead and wounded here.

We rumbled into a ditch as the driver's concentration lapsed for a moment. We slid against a tree, pushing a vehicle in front of us until it toppled to one side, and reached the open ground on the other side of the bridge. God bless our cross-country half-track radio truck!

We first discovered here – and that right unfriendly – that the Heubude Bridge had been made unusable by a bomb hit hours ago and was therefore closed. The sappers working on it and the military police assigned to its closure had been lying under cover as we drove across the Vistula without their permission.

Another bomber squadron approached us and plastered us with its machine guns, having already dropped its bombs, probably in the woods, which were swarming with refugees.

Where should a line of defence be established now that Danzig had been evacuated? Women, children, old folk, horses and carts were everywhere, and among them the fresh graves of those killed by the constant air attacks.

The Soviet bombers could hardly miss this enormous concentration of human beings in this tight area. A few of the people appeared to have already drawn a lesson from this, or they had been unable to find room to camp in the light woods among the dunes, and slit trenches had been dug here and there.

But we assembled, as ordered, behind the mighty dam that provided shelter and protection from the south and Danzig. One by one our few still mobile tanks trundled in. The radio could be switched off. We slept like logs on that night of 29/30 March. In the morning we awoke to an artillery barrage that covered us in dirt. We then dug out holes in the wide dam. There were infantry guards at the water's edge in front of us. We were in the second line as a counterattack reserve.

Everywhere the water formed the front line around us. At first this was a reassurance for us. On 27 March German engineers had been ordered to breach the Vistula dams and open the flood gates. All the land between Elbing and the Frisches Haff had thus been flooded and rendered impassable.

This, however, had the disadvantage that the vehicles were jammed into jumbled clumps in the dunes either side of the Vistula, so the Army ordered the destruction of all the vehicles without exception.

From the 4th Panzer Division we could see that these vehicles would certainly not be needed further in this island situation, but one objected strongly to destroying the fighting vehicles and complained to General von Saucken, who authorised the 4th Panzer Division to retain its reconnaissance vehicles, armoured personnel carriers, self-propelled guns and combat tanks with their workshops and support vehicles. Thus the 4th remained a Panzer Division until the very end.

Chapter 8

In the Danzig Meadows

Until 30 March it was possible to hold the Mottlau River line from Ohra to Neufahrwasser and thus secure the only still intact Vistula Bridge near Heubude for the flood of refugees and German troops and to steer them towards the wooded dunes near Krakau and Heubude. Despite considerable enemy interference, chaos was avoided.

But the busy shuttle service from Neufahrwasser to Hela had to be abandoned as the Soviets coming from Glettkau and Brösen occupied the other bank, and the harbour came within Soviet rifle range. There were still only a few refugees to be directed to Neufahr, where there were still some naval craft and the sapper ferries.

The incalculable mass of people of 31 March had greatly diminished overnight. Perhaps the people had been ordered on. Many of the more experienced people might well have thought that where the tanks were, the Ivans could not be far off. In our deathlike sleep we had experienced none of this. A warm soup with plenty of meat brought us a new lease of life.

On these first days of April things were relatively quiet. The whole of the flat landscape between the Vistula and the Baltic could be seen from the Danzig Heights as occasional, focussed artillery barrages showed. The soldiers of the Red Army took Danzig noisily and celebrated their success with vodka and music. We could hear the noise of their victory celebrations until the morning. Their loudspeaker propaganda came constantly across the harbour to our side: 'Soldiers of the German 2nd Army! Now you are in a trap, in a self-service prisoner of war camp.' Then they would play the Radetzky March, with many Red Army soldiers firing their weapons to its beat. Then came an announcement: 'Now follows an organ concert. On the organ, Joseph Stalin.' A rocket barrage no longer came as a surprise to us. Then followed the well-known quotations about immediate return to the homeland after the war, good handling and the retention of one's private possessions. Finally, they threatened us with total destruction if we did not believe them. Quite new in this propaganda game was that they now played day and night over their giant loudspeakers Marrika Röck's recording to us: '*In der Nacht ist der Mensch nicht gern alleine*' ('People do not like to be alone at night'). They must have captured the song in Danzig, as the film *Frau meiner Träume* (*Woman of my Dreams*) had been released in the cinemas there in January.

On the harbour mole directly opposite us were displayed the flags of the Soviet Union and the Free Germany National Committee. This alone was painful, but awareness of the atrocities and the orgies of hate to which those left behind in Danzig were being subjected, brought many to the brink of despair.

The political officer schooled for many years in hatred of the Germans in the 2nd Byelrussian Front opposite us, Major Lev Kopelev, 'Senior Instructor in deployment among enemy troops and enemy population', who at this time was arrested not far from us for 'lacking vigilance and having a bourgeois-humanitarian attitude in the form of sympathy for the Germans', wrote on p. 16 of his book *Aufbewahren für alle Zeit* (*Saving for Ever*) his thoughts on the inhuman behaviour in East and West Prussia:

What happened in East Prussia? Was such brutal behaviour by our troops really necessary and inevitable? Rape and robbery, are they necessary? Why must Poland and ourselves take East Prussia, Pomerania and Silesia? In his time Lenin rejected the Versailles Agreement, but this was worse than Versailles. In the newspapers and on the radio we call for a holy revenge. But what kind of avengers were these and on whom had they taken revenge? Why turn so many of our soldiers into kinds of bandits that gang-rape women and girls on the roadside in the snow, in passage ways, who beat the unarmed to death, destroying, ruining, burning everything they cannot take along with them, senselessly out of a pure sense of destruction. How has this become possible?

Have we been trained, we the political workers, journalists, writers – Ehrenburg and Simonov and hundreds of thousands of other industrious, ambitious but also talented agitators, teachers, instructors, as sincere preachers of 'holy revenge'?

We teach them to hate, convincing them that the German is already bad simply because he is a German, and we praise his murder in poems, prose and paintings. 'Daddy, hit the Germans!'

There was a time in which I was almost ashamed not to have a tally of beaten Germans.

And Major Kopelev, still alive in the West today, writes a lot more, he who had to suffer long years in Soviet punishment camps because he showed compassion for the German women and children, who out of pure lust for killing and at the behest of Ilya Ehrenberg and comrades were beaten and tortured. This should be remembered.

Also the Nobel Prize winner, Alexander Solschenizyn, in 1945 a captain in the Red Army engaged in the Kurischer Nehrung and arrested in February 1945 for bourgeois views, reported on p. 31 of the first part of his book *The Gulag Archipelago*:

Yes – After three weeks of war in Germany we knew exactly. If they were German girls, everyone had raped them and then could shoot them, and it had seemed almost a warlike act. If they were Poles or our own abducted Russian girls once could at least chase them naked across the fields and slap them on the bum, a game, nothing more. But the person concerned was the 'field and army wife' of the head of counterintelligence.

During the first days of April we lay on a kind of island between the two mouths of the Vistula and the Baltic Sea. On this 'waterfront' it was relatively quiet at first with occasional artillery and rocket salvo fire. Then suddenly on 4 April there was a tank alert. The Soviets were on the east bank near Neufahrwasser. The anti-aircraft battalion that had been stationed there had gone. It was unclear whether it had been surprised by the Soviets and overrun, or had decided to go over to them. With much luck, our tanks were able to force the Red Army soldiers back to the west bank. Thus for a short time they were further south on 'Heubude Island', as that piece of land was called.

Consequently, on 5 April the German troops had to withdraw behind the second arm of the Vistula near Neufähr to Bohnsack, from where the shuttle to Hela was removed to Schiewenhorst.

After the town and harbour of Gotenhafen had to be abandoned to the Soviets on 28 March following some bitter fighting, the refugee transports went from Oxhöft immediately north of there to Hela. The 7th Panzer Division, now under the command of our former regimental commander, Colonel Christern, fought a desperate battle against time supported by the naval artillery. The German troops formed a protective wall for the women and children, and all available shipping space was used to take them to Hela as quickly as possible.

As of 4 April all the refugees had been removed, General von Saucken, commander-in-chief of the German 2nd Army, contrary to Hitler's express orders, gave the codeword '*Walpurgisnacht*' for the evacuation of the Oxhöft fields. Continuing the fighting there had become pointless. The last vessel sailed at 0600 hours on 5 April. That afternoon the High Command's order for the evacuation of Oxhöft was received: too late.

Our tanks were brought quickly to the east bank of the Vistula arm by the engineers' special ferries with the Soviets hard on our heels. Our junior medical officer, who could not be despondent even in the most awkward situations, took out his accordion, sat on the last tank floating slowly over the river, and sang '*Eine Insel im Laufschritt verloren*' ('An island lost on the march') to the then popular tune on the Services' Radio '*Eine Insel aus Träumen geboren*' ('An island born of dreams').

Having crossed the second arm of the Vistula we promptly sat down again on a sandy island, as the mouth of the Vistula delta extended to a width of 60km from Neufahrwasser down to Elbing. We called this piece of land in the water between Schiewenhorst and Neufähr, the Vistula and the Baltic, 'Schnakenburg Island'.

Further inland, outside the range of the Soviet artillery, there was bustling activity everywhere, a sheer, incalculable mass of people. The confused dialects of people from all parts of the country made one think of the story of the building of the tower of Babel, not only because it was taking place between two areas of water. There was earnest shovelling and digging going on everywhere. Just about all the peoples of Europe were represented here.

I first encountered the thirty-two British officer prisoners of war, who about four weeks previously had come over to us in the Heiderode area, complying with the articles of war with white flags and spokesmen going ahead. They had credibly told us that they had been freed from German captivity in Schlossberg by Red Army soldiers and then transported East with an unknown destination. They had had no confidence in this release and had used a suitable opportunity to become independent and force their way through to the German front by night and fog. And they had pointedly, politely and correctly begged, in that fine English manner, to come back and stay with us. If necessary, they declared unasked, they would even be prepared to fight on the German side.

This offer had immediately given us a powerful boost in our despondency. Of course we took them on, genuinely sharing supplies and cigarettes.

The situation was then so confused that the British had to stay at our regimental command post until they could be taken to the rear. During this time we came to a good mutual understanding and made friends with some of them. Now they were waiting here, like the other hundred-thousand, for shipment to the West.

One thing that struck me was the French prisoners of war attached to nearly all the farming families from East and West Prussia, and who carefully looked after 'their families', making sure that they did not become separated from them in this turmoil. They were just about the only men with the treks if one does not count the old folk. They were especially good to the children, who clung to their 'Jean'. This could not be overlooked. For five years many Frenchmen had wanted to be with 'their own families'.

Somewhat apart from 'the simple folk', the reserved aristocracy of Reval and Riga were camping in fur coats with heavy boxes and ship's chests. They strutted around with their former servants that, in view of the completely altered social structure, no longer wanted to obey them as before.

A group of Polish women huddled in a hollow, apparently wanting to go to the West with us, perhaps because they feared the scorn of their victorious compatriots. In any case they were taciturn, only whispering occasionally and quietly among themselves.

Russian volunteers, former Red Army soldiers that still stood on our side, deliberated among themselves. In view of the obvious end in sight, they had to decide quickly, which way they would go. The situation was especially tragic for them.

And all these hundreds of thousands of soldiers and civilians, West and East Prussians, Lithuanians, Estonians and Letts, Pomeranians and Poles, British and French, all ate at our field kitchens from appropriated vats and even bricked-in bathtubs, and thanks to our extraordinarily good organisation, all were satisfied.

All the infantry horses, and also those from the refugee wagons that had been abandoned, made their way to the field kitchens. We ate them without knowing it. The care and feeding of the people herded together in the Vistula flats was a brilliant achievement.

And the second major achievement that we landlubbers were still only on the verge of taking in was the tireless commitment of the

German Navy and Merchant Navy. The men in blue uniforms brought ships of all sizes, ferries and boats of all kinds to extricate people from this witches' cauldron, first to Hela, where, following the loss of the harbours of Danzig and Gotenhafen, the big ships waited out at sea. From day to day the woods and dunes were noticeably emptier. There was absolutely no sign of panic. There was an unnatural quiet after the hectic weeks in Danzig.

This short breathing space was used to put the fighting units into order and to refill the depleted companies of Panzergrenadiers. Staffs and rear area services were disbanded, or at least reduced, and the men thus released assigned to the fighting units. It was now a question of life or death. Administration, reports and repairs were no longer required. There was also no longer either a front or a rear, the front was everywhere.

Our 1st Battalion, Panzer Regiment 35, still disposed of twenty battle-worthy vehicles. The crews of the shot-up tanks had fought in Danzig with submachine guns and panzerfausts, sacrificing themselves. Their losses had been extremely painful. Now, if they had not been wounded, they were allocated with the clerks and drivers, headquarters staff and mechanics to the panzergrenadier companies. For many of them this was equivalent to a death sentence, as they had no experience in the infantry role. There was only one comforting thought for them, they might receive a suitable wound for evacuation very soon and before it was too late, for the evacuation by sea of the wounded was still in process.

Some found a hearing from a generous medical officer for a hidden pain. Now and then a sympathetic medical orderly hung a wounded pass around the neck of an elderly senior corporal and provided the necessary documentation. It was known, and everyone knew that one could only leave alive with the requisite documentation, for the military police were pitiless, and manned all the control points. Several brave warriors that had tried to get through, despite all the warnings, found themselves hung from a branch with a notice on their stomachs: 'Sentenced to death for desertion'.

And then a rumour made the rounds, one that had already sprung up in mid-March. It was that 200 experienced tank men were to be taken by ship to Schleswig Holstein to take over some new tanks, but one heard nothing about what would follow. Only to get away from here! Get away from this hell! To get out from this mousetrap before it was finally sprung!

A competition over fate's favours began, a wooing of one's comrades and superiors. Who would be able to leave this witches' cauldron? What would be the grounds for selection?

And what everyone hoped for but no one believed became true overnight: 200 men from Panzer Regiment 35, experienced tank-crew men, would be provided with the essential documentation and would leave immediately for Hela according to a short and sober order from Division. Captain Küspert, commander of the disbanded 2nd Battalion, was designated commander of this group.

After some long discussion the wise decision was reached to send home over the Baltic above all last sons, fathers and married men. Naturally, this did not come about without little jealousies, pushing and shoving from those not on the list of 200. But the decision was then generally accepted as being quite correct.

And the lucky ones – those selected from among us candidates for death, as we saw it – were sent off equipped with proper marching orders, certified with seals and signatures. They scooted off in groups on foot and on commandeered bicycles. A race to the coast began. No one wanted to miss possibly the last chance for freedom and getting back to life.

Chapter 9

The Küspert Group

On 16 April 1945, full of hope and plans for the future, our 200 comrades from Panzer Regiment 35 joined 6,000 other people on board the cargo ship *Goya* that would take them away from the 'front without end' and back to life.

They took with them our best wishes and greetings to our loved ones. We were left behind with bitterness in our hearts and very little hope for the future while in constant touch with death.

They stretched out their hands to the homeland and for the gift of life once more. Then they received a severe blow and 6,000 people sank in the water!

The Sinking of the *Goya*
The motor ship *Goya* was a modern and fast twin-screw freighter with a displacement of 5,230 tons, built in 1942. Quite bizarre camouflage paintwork made her almost unrecognisable.

The 16 April 1945 had already begun badly for the crew with a dawn attack by Soviet bombers. The ship's anti-aircraft guns fired madly, but the *Goya* was hit during the fourth attack. A bomb struck the foredeck, ripping it up and wounding the gun crew, and Captain Plünnecke was hit by a bomb splinter.

Despite the hole on the main deck, the ship still remained navigable. At 0900 hours it began loading refugees, the wounded and soldiers from tenders providing a shuttle service. The whole day ferries and tenders lay alongside the *Goya,* but Soviet aircraft were attacking constantly, causing distress to those on board and embarking, causing some panic for a while, and there were some painful losses.

According to the ship's manifest, at about 1900 hours there were 6,000 people on board, including 1,800 soldiers, but the manifest was incomplete as more forced their way aboard. It was finally accepted that there were at least 7,000 people aboard the *Goya*.

She cast off at about 2000 hours Summer Time with the advent of darkness, and formed up with the other ships for the journey to the West. In convoy with her were the two smaller ships, *Kronenfels* and *Aegiav,* with minesweepers M256 and M328 as escorts. The *Goya* led in the northernmost position.

Upon reaching the open sea, the people on board relaxed and the Soviet air attacks dwindled, but the fear of submarines and mines increased. The ship was overloaded, and the lower gangways and stairwells fully crammed. The air was thick enough to cut with a knife and it was almost impossible to get on deck. The speed of the convoy was set at 9 sea miles per hour, as they had to conform with the slowest ship.

At 2203 the lookout reported a silhouette to starboard. The M328 fired flares and the silhouette disappeared. The order was given 'Don life jackets!', but there were only 1,500 available.

At about 2230 hours the *Kronenfels* slowed down and stopped shortly afterwards with engine trouble. The other ships in the convoy gathered round and waited. On the *Kronenfels* they feverishly tried to repair the damage with the tools they had, and eventually succeeded. Meanwhile, the two escort vessels circled round the stricken ship. At about 2330 hours the convoy, which was then off Rixhöft at the base of the Putziger Nehrung, resumed its course.

At this juncture no one knew that the submarine L-3, commanded by Lieutenant Commander V.K. Konovalov, had been following the convoy for a considerable time.

At 2345 hours the *Goya* was shaken by two massive explosions. The ship immediately rolled sharply to one side. It was badly ripped in the bows and sinking rapidly astern. The lighting was extinguished with a blow. Orders rang out in the darkness: 'Save yourselves if you can!' The water rushed noisily into the interior of the ship and the first people jumped overboard.

Indescribable panic broke out below deck. Hundreds had been badly injured. All rushed for the stairs, wanting to go up. Many were knocked down and trampled underfoot in the impetuous pushing from behind, especially children. The ship sank further aft and was already partly submerged by the water. Even before the lifeboats could be launched, the *Goya* broke into two parts, which began sinking quite quickly. In no time at all the people on deck were up to their waists in water. Then, as the masts tipped over, many left the ship and swam for their lives.

A tongue of flame as high as a house rose from the fatefully damaged *Goya,* and several explosions followed in the interior of the ship. Then

19 January 1945. The voyage from Kurland to West Prussia. Loading the troopship *Preussen* at Libau. Vehicles and heavy weapons were left in Kurland; only special vehicles and radio sets were taken.

The convoy gathers before departure. Bad weather prevented attacks by Soviet bombers. The ice floes show how cold it was.

A submarine returning from a patrol.

At sea in dense fog. The deck is crowded with packing cases.

A tank crew at sea. From left to right: First Lieutenant Peters, Second Lieutenant Fintelmann (in lifejacket), Captain Prast.

Late January 1945. Without delay we marched south through the snow, past endless lines of refugees fleeing to the Baltic Sea.

February 1945. A Panzer IV knocked out and swamped beside the road after the attack at Blondmin.

A damaged Panzer being recovered by three half-tracks.

The successful Panzer IV known as 'Molch'. In this tank Second Lieutenant Gaf Rudiger von Moltke knocked out thirty-five Soviet tanks in two months. Moltke stands on the right, with Second Lieutenant Klemm.

24 February 1945. At last twenty-seven Panzer Vs – Panthers – arrived from Kurland. Twenty-three were assigned to Panzer Regiment 35. South of Stargard they went into action for the first time.

As we discovered in Kurland, with the Panther's powerful main gun we had nothing to fear from the Soviet Josef Stalin tanks.

The Panther had a weight of 44.8 tons and as armament three machine guns and a 7.5cm main gun. The frontal armour was 80mm thick, side armour 45mm. The maximum speed was 46kmh.

The Panther was comparatively unreliable, but the maintenance service was well organised and experienced at Panzer Regiment 35. Here a mechanic is delivering replacement parts for a Panther that has broken down.

A Soviet T-34/85 knocked-out by a direct hit on the turret.

A knocked-out Soviet Josef Stalin tank. The force of the explosion in the crew compartment has blown the turret off the hull. The Joseph Staling had a tree-like 12.2cm main gun.

The command tank of the first division of Panzer Regiment 35. Note the additional aerials. The main gun was a dummy. In the turret is Hauptmann Kastner.

Early March 1945. The civilian population had to leave their homeland in a hurry. The Nazi party agencies left them in the dark about the seriousness of the situation. The Wehrmacht helped the refugees where it could.

Red Army troops advanced relentlessly along the Baltic coast, using heavy artillery to shell the harbours. A dramatic race to Danzig was under way.

Soviet bombers attacked columns of vehicles and refugees.

From three directions, streams of refugees converged on Karthaus. The bombers circled over the columns, bombing and strafing, and the casualties among the refugees and the soldiers were heavy. Here a soldier drives a wagon loaded with fleeing women and children.

An anxious woman glances back as the soldier with her in the wagon searches the sky for attacking aircraft.

The fear shows on all the faces.

These women and children walk north towards Danzig and Gdingen. The road behind them is choked with carts and horses.

The ruins of Danzig, 30 March 1945. The Frauengasse, the Marienkirche, Staatstheate, the Gorsse Muhle, the fish market with the Church of St Johann in the background, the Brigittenkirsche.

The heavy cruiser *Prinz Eugen,* along with the battleship *Silesia* and light cruiser *Leipzig,* gave support with her guns to the fleeing civilians and defending soldiers.

The liner *Goya* in a bizarre camouflage paint scheme. On 16 April 1945 the *Goya,* with some 7,000 people on board, was sunk near Hela by a Soviet submarine. Only 183 people were saved. This was one of the largest maritime disasters of all time.

The Vistula ferry operated day and night despite artillery fire and air raids.

The Vistula is just over half a kilometre wide. Again and again Soviet fighter aircraft attacked the ferry.

In the late afternoon of 8 May 1945, the last day of the war, the ferry sailed, laden with soldiers, out the Vistula mouth and across the Baltic Sea to Kiel.

On 27 May 1945, on the orders of the army, the locks on the Vistula were opened, flooding the Elbinger Werder to protect the German troops until they reached the Vistula lagoon. The 7th Infantry Division stubbornly defended this water barrier.

Lieutenant-General of Panzer Troops Dietrich von Saucken, commander of the 2nd Army. He organised the evacuation of the refugees and wounded, but considered it his duty to stay with his soldiers on Hela and near the Vistula. He was captured by the Soviets and spent ten years in captivity.

Lieutenant-General Blemens Betzel, commander of the 4th Panzer Division, was killed in the fight for Danzig on 27 March 1945 at Olivaer Tor.

Colonel Ernst W. Hoffmann, commander of the 12th Panzergrenadier Regiment, led the 4th Panzer Division after the death of General Betzel.

Colonel Hans Christern, commander of the 35 Panzer Regiment, was entrusted with the leadership of the 7th Panzer Division in Gdingen following the wounding of General Mauss.

Hans Schaüfler, the author of this book, was born in 1912. From 1939 to 1945 he served in the 4th Panzer Division. During the campaigns in Kurland and West Prussia he was regimental intelligence officer in Panzer Regiment 35. After the Armistice on 8 May 1945 he escaped from Soviet custody, sailing from the mouth of the Vistula over the Baltic Sea to Sweden and from there to Schleswig-Holstein where he became an English prisoner of war.

everything happened very, very quickly. Within a few minutes both halves of the ship vanished under water.

The survivors that had been driven into the water saw the shape of a surfaced submarine briefly. The area was more than full of screaming people, debris from the ship and corpses. Women cried and men swore. At this time of year the water was still ice-cold and quickly turned their bodies numb, rendering them powerless. Most of the people were only thinly clothed, for it had been very warm in the press aboard the *Goya*.

Shattering cries for help rang out through the night. The swimmers clutched at every support, one pulling another down into the depths. Here and there blinked the yellow lights on the rubber life-rafts that had been switched on by coming into contact with the water, making this terrible scene even more gruesome.

Soldiers called out for their comrades, trying to get together in a life-raft. Some life-rafts tipped over from overloading. A bitter struggle for the hand grips was in process, the thin pieces of rope that could mean survival. Latecomers were driven off with kicks and blows by those there ahead of them or were pulled down into the depths. The brutal elementary right of the survival of the fittest was being implemented. There were fewer swimmers with every minute, and soon there was no dispute with those hanging on to the floats. The cries from the water became weaker and weaker, then there was a gurgle, and that was all.

Two hours later, in the very last minutes, the escort minesweeper M328 fished out of the water those still surviving close by. Half-frozen and completely hypothermic, those saved were wrapped in warm blankets and brought down below decks for medical treatment. Just one-hundred of them could be brought back to life. A motor boat rescued another eighty-three survivors. All were later transferred to the *Kronenfels,* which took them on to Copenhagen, together with those people already on board.

Only 183 people survived, including 7 comrades from Panzer Regiment 35's 200. Well over 6,000 people had gone down with the *Goya.*

Hundreds had been killed by the two torpedo hits, ripped and torn by the pressure. Thousands drowned from the water pouring in through these holes. Within 20 minutes the equivalent of a small town had ceased to exist. Nobody notified their next of kin. The victims of the *Goya* were on the terrible lists of war casualties recorded as 'missing'. The news of the sinking of the *Goya* failed to reach the fighting front on the Vistula. We all thought our comrades had got through safely. It was years later that we heard of the greatest catastrophe at sea in people's memory.

Joachen Hannemann was one of the seven saved from our Panzer Regiment 35, and his personal experience is given here to reinforce the forgoing account:

16th April 1945 – shortly after 2000 hours the *Goya* departed Hela with 6,488 refugees, wounded and soldiers. Two mines-weepers escorted the convoy.

We of Panzer Regiment 35 were accommodated in the lower cabins amidships. Everywhere in the passageways, cabins and holds stood, sat and lay women, children, wounded and soldiers. One could hardly move. It was hot and the air scarce. Once more I made my way up to top deck in order to get some fresh air, which probably saved my life.

The night was starry and the sea calm. Outside it was very cold. Shortly before midnight – I was already back on deck – there were two dull blows, and the ship rose up. Gigantic columns of water went into the black night sky and crashed down on the deck. Suddenly the lights went out. Panic broke out below deck on the *Goya*. On the staircases to the lower decks a fearful scene evolved as a fight for life and death broke out. What occurred down in the interior of the ship was beyond anyone's experience. Water poured into the vast holes where the torpedoes had struck. The ship broke in two in the middle and sank very quickly. The raging of the masses of water was frightening.

As there was nothing to keep me on the ship, I jumped over the railings into the icy cold flood of the Baltic. A giant wave carried me off. Suddenly a life-raft shot up in front of me that presumably had been released by the water pressure from the sinking *Goyav.* Later there was a whole group of people hanging on to the raft.

We fought the waves in the ice-cold water despairingly for two whole hours. We were completely exhausted when a naval boat came and took us aboard. I counted 172 people saved. More than 6,000 went down into the depths with the *Goya,* thinking that they had left all danger behind them.

In the afternoon all the shipwrecked people were transferred from the naval boat to the freighter *Kronenfels,* which took us on to Copenhagen. Of the 200 strong Küspert group only seven comrades survived. Apart from myself they were: Sergeant Major Kurt Moser, Sergeant Wehner, Sergeant Gross, Corporal Jung, Senior Corporal Veit and Corporal Burckhardt.

Chapter 10

Waiting at the Mouth of the Vistula

The Vistula Canal of 1840, which cut through to the west and caused the arm of the Vistula near Neufahrwasser to be downgraded to 'the dead Vistula', had been the true mouth of the Vistula since this adjustment a century ago. The wide river pours stolidly into the Baltic between Schiewenhorst and Nickelswalde, and mighty tongues of sand dunes escort it a bit further into the open sea.

The river is far too wide for bridges at this point, so there is a capacious river ferry that can take a whole company of infantry across in one go. It operates to and fro between both these places on the river. The intrepid men that operate this most important traffic link, are worthy of the highest praise today as they handled this quite lively business over the Vistula during air attacks and under artillery fire. We old front-line soldiers avoided those allergic points on the water that attracted Soviet aircraft and provoked their artillery, but the men up there in the glass-fronted wheelhouse made their way across the water unperturbed. And finally, right at the end, they set off, fully laden with soldiers, all the way over the Baltic to Kiel. Hats off to the Schiewenhorst ferry and its brave and intrepid crew!

The engineers had constructed landing stages right and left along the bank from where naval ferries and sapper landing craft conveyed refugees and wounded across the Danzig Bight to Hela, where the big transports lay in the roadstead. They would not and could not enter Hela's little harbour, for it lay on the landward side with the Soviets right opposite. There were still hundreds of thousands awaiting shipment, and every day more arrived over the spit of the Frische Nehrung, camping in blocks of 1,000 persons in foxholes in the pinewoods either side of the mouth of the Vistula. Despite all precautions and care, they still suffered losses from Soviet air attacks. Bombers and fighters were in the air without a break, being replaced at night by the slow-flying biplanes, for which the soldiers had so many apt names: 'Runway Jodellers', 'Night Owls', 'Natashas', 'Fog Crows', and so on. They found their way here easily, the white sandbanks of the Nehrung providing good orientation for them.

Out there on the Baltic, about 5 or 10km offshore, remained the German Navy's three warships *Prim Engen, Leipzig* and *Schlesien,* but they were more decorative than really effective, for they only had very little ammunition available and were no longer taking part in the land battle. They were running targets for Soviet air attacks, but the ships' anti-aircraft guns were so astonishingly good that the Soviets were unable to score an effective direct hit, although they switched to bombers, fighters and torpedo planes, losing quite a few aircraft. Finally they gave up, leaving the warships alone.

However, their presence gave us a little moral support, and we did not feel completely abandoned. Somehow the scene was impressive, even for the Soviets. We sought the protection of their heavy guns and the Red Army soldiers avoided them if possible, even if the stocks of shells in their magazines were limited.

On 14 April, Marshal Vassilevsky's divisions had attacked in Samland with dreadful force after having occupied Königsberg on the 10th, but penetration of the Frische Nehrung near Pilau was checked. General von Saucken had now assumed command of the German 4th Army.

On 20 April our 4th Panzer Division was tasked with forming an armoured battle group. Panzer Regiment 12, the 2nd Battalion Armoured Artillery Regiment 103, and the remaining fighting vehicles of Panzer Regiment 35 were assigned to it. The group was commanded by Major von Heyden and was directly subordinated to the 2nd Army.

But the grenadiers and the artillery were still in action west of the Vistula opening. They had first to be got out then brought across the river. This was all very time-consuming as there were no bridges, and the two ferry terminals at Schievenhorst and Schönbaumerweide were prime targets for Soviet air attacks.

Armoured Reconnaissance Battalion 4 was put on alert on 23 April. Despite the strong counter traffic from uncontrolled refugee movement, within a few hours traffic was diverted to the other end of the Nehrung opposite Pilau exactly at the time when the Soviets wanted to attack the Nehrung with landing craft and speed boats. The concentrated firepower of the armoured reconnaissance and personnel-carrying vehicles forced them back into the water with heavy losses.

The armoured group assembled in the dunes east of the Vistula on 24 April, and was quickly deployed in the Frische Nehrung in the area of Kahlberg, Liep and Pröbbernau, where a Soviet landing was expected. What luck that they still had these armoured fighting vehicles!

The Frische Nehrung, where we as the Army's counterattack reserve lay, is a 65km-long wooded strip of dunes between the Baltic and Frisches Haff lagoon, which is at times only 800m wide and about 5 to 10m above the level of the Baltic.

In the months of January to March this tongue of land had been the escape route taken by thousands of East Prussians. Now the remains of the defeated German 4th Army were pressing southwestwards towards the mouth of the Vistula. The rough sandy road had disintegrated beyond recognition and the loose dune sand was full of foxholes like a lunar landscape.

Numerous defensive positions carefully constructed by the Organisation Todt a long time ago ran from the Frisches Haff to the Baltic. Unfortunately, they had been designed to face west, towards Danzig.

Chapter 11

That Was Hell

Fighting Retreat on the Frische Nehrung

It was not long before the attacking Soviets reached the area of Neukrug with an unimaginable commitment of resources and ammunition. The 4th Panzer Division's armoured group took an active part in this battle that was to prove so costly for us.

This dance of death began furiously for me. The staff of the 1st Battalion, Panzer Regiment 35, had moved to a lonely forester's house in a thick pine wood near Vöglers, where we made ourselves comfortable. A tracked motorcycle from the supply unit had brought along with the coffee the first forces mail again, which had been held up somewhere. For me there was the Christmas parcel from my young wife that had not reached me in Kurland. It contained Christmas biscuits that had long crumbled into dust and a long-life cake that, despite the long journey, was still edible, and a pair of hand-knitted knee warmers.

Whilst these things and thoughts pleased me, I knew that these would be the last signs of life from home for a long time as I heard artillery fire coming from a corner over the lagoon from where there had been nothing before. During years of war one had developed an ear and feeling for whether their gun barrels were directed at one's own position. We scraped around, although we were surrounded by brick walls, changed our minds and vanished outside into the foxholes, of which there were so many that had been dug by others.

And we were right in doing so, for the shells struck very close to us, one shell scoring a direct hit on the forester's lodge. These were mighty big shells that had been sent across the lagoon. Not a mouse could have survived in the lodge. Even my Christmas packet lying on a table was ripped into a thousand pieces. I found only one of the knee warmers knitted by my wife under bits of wall. I do not know why, but I took it along with me through all the perils I was to endure. I still have it as a souvenir of the Frisches Haff in 1945.

We had thought that an increase in the inferno that we had

experienced in Danzig was impossible. We learned otherwise.

These final days of this unhappy war, about which no front-line correspondent has written, were the worst to bear because of crippling uncertainty, gloomy despair gnawing at our hearts and the merciless fight for life which feasted greedily on the last strength in our emaciated bodies.

Unarmed soldiers in torn uniforms with dulled eyes in grey faces staring with horror hastened past day and night to the rear along the bumpy log track of the spit road. These were the survivors of the defeated German 4th Army from East Prussia, Samland and Königsberg who had somehow escaped death over the Frisches Haff lagoon.

Wounded and ever more wounded came, their bandages black with blood. But not one of them would let us replace their dressings. Not once did they even stop for a sip of water from the water bottles offered to them, for a bit of bread, for a cigarette, for a short rest. What a terrible time they must have had!

Back, Back! Don't lose any time, away from the storm of lead and steel, away from this pitiless front. That was their only thought. They did not know that this was a front without an end.

The Soviets drummed down on the narrow, in parts 800m wide, strip of land almost ceaselessly with their light artillery, called by the troops *Ratschbum* because of the sound of their firing. Dozens of rocket launchers, known as Stalin Organs, and hundreds of mortars of all calibres fired from close up to the strip, and we could do nothing about them. At least 180 guns, from 122mm upwards, were firing across the strip. At intervals Soviet gunboats joined in from out at sea. Numerous enemy tanks: T-34s, Joseph Stalins, American Shermans and assault guns with reinforced front armour called Rambucks made life difficult for us. Several shock anti-tank guns fired from along the coast at the spit road.

Our panzer battalion was in a night and fog operation on 29 April in support of the tightly enclosed Armoured Reconnaissance Battalion 4 near Vöglers. Stage by stage in an expensive defensive battle we reached Kahlberg, which was lost on 3 May. Now Panzergrenadier Regiment 12 was also engaged.

Although Pröbbernau had to be abandoned to the Soviets on 5 May, the Red Army divisions had been unable to overrun the German troops so far. On the night of 5/6 May we lost the former regimental command tank in close-quarter fighting, being unable to fight with its mock cannon. As there was still radio equipment on board, it had to be shot on fire from one of our own tanks. In its place, the divisional communications battalion gave us a radio-equipped armoured personnel carrier.

On 7 May we defended ourselves in the area of Bodenwinkel at the southern end of the Frische Nehrung spit. We still had eighty survivors from the 1st Battalion, Panzer Regiment 35, with twelve broken-backed fighting vehicles with little fuel and only a few shells, and they were now deployed within the framework of the 7th Bavarian Infantry Division, which had withstood all Soviet attacks until now.

The positions here were well constructed. Every 4 to 5km there was a trench cutting through from the lagoon to the Baltic Sea. Two, at the most three, of these positions were occupied as a precaution. The Soviets methodically destroyed these trenches with their numerous heavy weapons. The tree bursts were frightful. These were shells with highly sensitive fuses that would explode at the slightest touch of a twig. Their whirling splinters fanning downwards made every movement outside a protective trench or a tank a gamble with death. The badly wounded could only be carried away by fresh victims. Pity those that had to be with an unfamiliar unit!

The May sky was a deep blue, the weather cruelly beautiful. So by day and also every night there was hardly an hour without a Soviet bomber howling over the treetops. Completely without a break, from early dawn until last light, the fighter aircraft crossed over, shot and hunted over the tops of the pines. Their rockets hissed into our ranks, into the gun positions, everywhere where there was a sign of life to alert them. Cannon and machine-gun shots whipped into the golden sand, trees splintered and tree tops broke, and then the next dozen were there. The anti-aircraft guns did not fire, having been silenced by the fighters.

Without any support, forgotten by God and ignored by the whole world, the survivors of the German 2nd Army conducted an incomparably desperate battle. What all knew was that we no longer fought for the 'Fatherland', not to win a battle, we stood solely alone on the Frische Nehrung because at the mouth of the Vistula, near Schiewenhorst, behind our backs were tens of thousands of women and children waiting for ships to take them to safety, first to Hela. In the last days 30,000 people were being taken away every day. Now the front here had to hold or bend and break.

And then the light humming of the Boston bombers, the 'greetings from America'. Twenty – forty – sixty – and then the roaring. Minute-long cracks – minute-long bangs. The earth shook and the ground swayed. Seconds became eternity. A giant cloud of dust rose out of the wood, darkening the sun, and with it the bloodcurdling cries of the injured and dying: 'Medic! Medic!'

These almost animal cries for help, these gurgling groans and the drawn-out suffocating is something I would like those responsible in the corridors of power to have to listen to. Then there would assuredly be no further wars without end on our earth.

It was enough to drive one crazy, to despair, having to bear witness to this without being able to do anything about it. But we knew that we had to hold on, we needed no orders.

A rumour went round that we, the armoured group, were to be the very last to be able to leave here. On the night of 9/10 May a warship would take us on board. So, in three day's time. Three days, 72 endlessly long hours. But what were 72 hours after nearly four years of war in the East?

Three times, four times, five times, one after the other, the Soviets attacked with heavy artillery barrages. They were convinced that they had extinguished all signs of life among the pine trees. But heavy defensive fire still met them from these trenches that had become the graves of many.

Once the foremost positions had been bled white, the front had to be pulled back to the next, already occupied line, because the hail of fire simply failed to ease up to enable reinforcements and ammunition to be brought forward. But the front as such held. Nowhere did the Soviets break through.

Our tanks performed magnificently. For ten days on end they had been in action around the clock. This sandy woodland was completely unsuitable for tank warfare. Nevertheless, they were always there to provide the infantry with moral support at critical moments. At times they constituted the only defence.

At about 1500 hours on 7 May all dispensable soldiers from our Panzer Regiment 35 were conveyed from Nickelswalde to Hela, having had to wait 30 hours for a ferry at the mouth of the Vistula. Only eight tank crews, a small maintenance team and a wireless troop remained. Three of the tanks were in full fighting order, and the five immobilised tanks were towed into prepared positions and buried up to their turrets in the Russian style to act as gun bunkers for the small bridgehead planned for 10 May.

We listened constantly to the transmission of foreign radio stations to keep informed of events here and in Germany. Thus we had also learned of the ceasefire talks in progress with the Western Allies on 3 May and that the guns had become silent on the Western Front at 0800 hours on 5 May. We were convinced that now all shipping would be sent to the East and take us soldiers back home now that the last of the refugees had reached the West on 6 May.

No ships had left here during the period 1 to 5 May. On 28 April, Vice-Admiral Thieze, the naval commander of the Eastern Baltic, had gone to Hela to confer with Colonel Schoepffer, the 2nd Army's delegate for refugee evacuation. About 200,000 people had congregated on the peninsula over the last days and every night another 30,000 arrived from the mouth of the Vistula as the ferry service worked flat out. On 3 May Vice-Admiral Thieze had sent the following message to the German Admiralty: 'As a result of the almost complete cessation of eastern convoy traffic from Hela, over 200,000 people have gathered here. Request immediate generous despatch of shipping for their transportation. 2 and 3 May only one steamer either day to the west. Assistance urgently required.'

What we did not yet know was that British bomber squadrons had systematically bombed the anchored German merchant ships in the Kiel and Lübecker Bights, sinking twenty-three of them and severely damaging eight others, including the anchored ocean liners *Cap Arkona* and *Deutschland* and the smaller *Thielbeck* flying the white flag.

And this was just at the time when the talks on the cessation of the fighting had almost reached a definitive point. Many refugees that thought they were really in safety at last after their arduous flight were killed on the ships.

Later on, after our flight, we were accommodated for two months at Sierksdorf, where we were able to learn all the details on the spot, and it was difficult to understand the behaviour of the British.

On 5 May the German Admiralty sent all available ships to the East at full speed to evacuate the troops still in Kurland, at Hela and at the mouth of the Vistula. Thus 23,700 from Kurland and 63,000 from Hela were brought to the West between 5 and 9 May.

At about 2300 hours on 7 May we heard from a foreign broadcast that Germany had capitulated unconditionally on all fronts. Naturally, we did not believe this, for it would mean that we who had held out on the spit would be punished with Soviet captivity. Certainly we had had to live with these thoughts over the past weeks, but now the frightening reality was so close that it sent shivers down our spines.

There was still a faint hope. The Divisional staff knew nothing about the surrender in the East. We, the last ten men of Panzer Regiment 35, carefully concocted plans, huddled even more closely together, thought about this, discussed that and took a number of precautions in case. We even sent liaison officers each equipped with a radio to a naval ship and to a ferry. We did not want to give up. Not yet!

Chapter 12

The End on the Vistula

When the sun rose blood-red out of the Baltic on 8 May, it showed us, the last soldiers on the Frische Nehrung spit, clearly and unmistakably that our fate was already decided. The warships at the mouth of the Vistula that had still provided a glimmer of hope for us had steamed away under cover of the night.

A beautiful May day bloomed over us, but doubt gnawed at our innermost feelings. A light wind from the east played with the tree tops, but the wind reeked of burning and blood, of death and corpses, of gunpowder and decay. We felt unutterably abandoned and betrayed. Even our opponents were hardly firing at us anymore. The spit, the Vistula embankments, everything had become so empty overnight.

The last lines of defence, the little bridgehead in which with so much effort our tanks had been towed and dug in, were no longer guarded. The tanks were to be destroyed. Only the three still mobile were to be retained. The released tank crews would be embarked with the workshop team and the radio troop. Another glimmer of light: a ship would still be sent.

I checked the radio equipment again, for the signals warrant officer responsible, Schmidt, had been killed a few days earlier. Explosions were occurring everywhere in the woods. Towing vehicles, guns and combat vehicles of all kinds were being blown up in accordance with orders. A shattering experience, but everyone wanted to clear the decks, everyone wanted to be able to leave immediately, everyone wanted to find a little hope.

At 1400 hours I received instructions from the battalion adjutant, Lieutenant Grigat, to march immediately to the mouth of the Vistula with the five tank crews and the other people, twenty-eight men in all. Our wireless armoured personnel carrier was already located there and was in contact with the ferry. There was something in the air, whatever it was.

What then occurred on the banks of the Vistula was most

disheartening. The ferries that should have taken us to Hela were already loaded. They were not coming back and were on their way to Kiel. Some small vessels still lay in the middle of the river, but meanwhile thousands of soldiers had gathered on the beach.

At 1700 hours it was confirmed by radio what had long been in everyone's mouth: 'Today at midnight cessation of hostilities – unconditional surrender.' Nobody said it out aloud, but it was written on everyone's face. The trap had been sprung and with it our dreams of returning home!

Yet, despite everything, perhaps for the last time in the history of our people, that renowned German discipline, Prussian discipline and order, but above all the comradeship that had developed in six hard years of war was displayed here.

Although everyone in the endless queue of those waiting knew that no further ships could be expected, that the two anchored in the middle of the Vistula could not take everyone, there was no tumult, no panic on the provisional landing stages. A couple of rear services soldiers that tried to work their way forward surreptitiously were quickly brought to their senses with elbows, not a word being said.

One of the two ships lay on our eastern side of the Vistula. The survivors of our Armoured Reconnaissance Battalion 4 were loaded on board it. I had express orders to accompany the tank men, but the radio armoured personnel carrier attached to us still stood on the bank with four men. The radios were still on 'receive' and were in communication with the Grigat Group, the very last unit of Panzer Regiment 35.

The commander of the Armoured Reconnaissance Battalion, Major von Gaupp, waved to me again to come aboard the ship. The four radio operators were still engaged. I stood undecided on the beach. Then I went back to the radio crew. I was ashamed of myself for having thought about leaving them here to their fate.

The driver, Senior Corporal Eckstein, who was busying himself with a machine gun, addressed me moist-eyed with a hoarse voice: 'Lieutenant, I don't know what I would have done if you had left us alone here. This last disappointment after everything would have been more than I could bear.'

The last ship sailed out of the mouth of the Vistula at 1820 hours completely overloaded. The soldiers were hanging on like bunches of grapes to everything that offered a hold. And they waved to us, those left behind.

A whistling in the earphones gave us a shock. A transmission!

Quickly we decoded it: 'Destroy vehicles and equipment. You are released from your oaths of allegiance. Try and break out however you can, ceasefire at midnight. End.' We acknowledged, but the radio was silent. These few words hit us like the blows of a hammer. If only they had come a couple of hours earlier!

Those that had been waiting had long since left, prepared to meet their fate alone, while we still stood undecided with our vehicle on the bank of the Vistula, looking at the completely empty fairway in which not even a plank floated.

We did not completely give up, and at 1900 hours we found an abandoned inflatable dinghy in the riverbank undergrowth. We quickly contacted the rearguard of a reconnaissance battalion at the extreme tip of the point who were preparing two engineer assault boats for the trip to Hela. Again a tiny flash of light; they promised to tow us in our dinghy.

At 2000 hours a respectable motorboat pulled up close alongside us, making us hopeful once more. I asked politely and modestly if I and my four men could go along with them. There was plenty of room, as I could see at a glance. But the unfriendly gentlemen did not deign to reply. They moved on, leaving us behind like stupid kids.

It was getting dark and we had become quite despondent when a small motorboat puttered up. A major was standing on the deck and waved me across. Embarrassedly he asked me if I could find my way across the Baltic with a motorboat. I hadn't the slightest idea, being a landsman by nature, but I could not say no to this man whom heaven had sent at the last minute. I pulled myself together and looked him fully in the face. "Of course I can, Major!'

To validate my claim I showed him the Russian field compass on my wrist, which looked very nautical.

Before the good man knew it, my four radio operators were already on the boat and vanished below deck. We five had immediately realised that this was fate's last helping hand stretched out to us and that we had to grab hold of it quickly and securely before it slipped from our grasp.

It was 2145 hours, as we passed through the mouth of the Vistula on our way to Hela, and it was already becoming dark. The first 'Night Owl' was already in the sky dropping flares and the occasional bomb.

The spit behind us grew smaller. We could still see the light-blue crowns of the pines on the darkening horizon. Like the wide open jaws of a crocodile, the sandbanks of the Vistula yawned behind us well out into the Baltic. I had the frightening feeling that they would snap shut before we got out of range.

Our motor boat, called *Zander,* really only had room for five passengers, and with fifteen men it was fully overloaded, but the main thing was that we were afloat. The sea was heaving slightly. The small, about 6m-long vessel was jumping from wave to wave like a high-spirited foal and the first men were seasick.

We could see the occasional flashes of exploding shells and bombs in the distance, behind us on the Vistula, but particularly more so ahead of us on the Hela peninsula. Searchlights showed the way for the Sewing Machines, the other name for the Night Owls, and parachute flares dangled over the sea.

We ran aground at 2300 hours. A narrow, barely discernible strip of land stretched out ahead of us in the sea. It must have been the Putziger spit. Actually we only wanted to get as far as here, but it was unnaturally quiet, so uninviting that we preferred to go round Hela in a wide curve to size up the other side. We went on and on.

Then a new day began. It was 9 May and 0130 hours. Behind us lay Hela, the ceasefire and surrender. Before us was the wide open Baltic. Before us was also an unknown future, full of dangers perhaps, but also full of hope. Our boat was small and certainly not built for a trip on the open sea but, nevertheless, we wanted to try it, for it was our only chance of escaping Soviet captivity. We were unanimous in our decision to flee over the Baltic.

Chapter 13

Flight Over the Baltic

For most of us landlubbers this was our first big trip on the sea, nevertheless we wanted to try it. We therefore took a northwesterly course, purely by feeling and a little according to my compass, although with all the iron on board, the compass was not to be trusted. Of course we had no map.

We wanted first to head for the Danish island of Bornholm, then perhaps even to Kiel if we could manage it with the boat. None of our crew had any acquaintance with the sea or a motorboat, but none had the least reservation about this journey, which could prove a fatal adventure for us.

At 0400 hours we changed course to due west. It began to get light. The Baltic was as flat as a mirror. A motorboat approached us. For a few minutes we did not know what to do, but then we saw German soldiers on deck. But our joy was short-lived when we realised that this was the boat that had rejected us yesterday. We tolerated its company, even though our hearts were against it, out of sheer self preservation. In an emergency one could call on the other for assistance.

At 0530 hours another boat appeared motionless on the sea. The crew waved at us. We could not believe our eyes – Colonel Hoffmann, the commander of our 4th Panzer Division, and Captain Illiger, the commander of our Armoured Signals Battalion 79, were on board. Apart from this there was a naval lieutenant and a young sailor. Their engine had broken down. The navigational problem appeared to be resolved now that we had sailors with us.

The four shipwrecked climbed aboard the *Seeadler,* as the unfriendly people's boat was called, that had turned away from us so brusquely yesterday and imposed themselves on us today. We could see that there was plenty of room on their boat.

At about 1000 hours we saw a lot of smoke behind us. Then we saw a big convoy moving majestically on a westerly course. We were convinced that they were the last transports from Kurland or Hela. We would follow them.

Then at about 1030 hours the *Seeadler* suffered a damaged clutch that brought it to a halt. It was discovered that the drive shaft was broken. So we took the big boat in tow, wanting to hand over the people to the convoy. *Zander* could now only make half speed, and we reckoned that, providing everything went well, it would take three days at this rate to reach Kiel. With difficulty, but bravely, the 65 PS engine pounded away. We jogged along about a kilometre south of the convoy and tried hard not to lose contact.

At about 1300 hours grey clouds suddenly swept across the Baltic and a bad storm arose. The *Zander* swung about madly and the *Seeadler* jerked on its towrope. We quickly learned how to manoeuvre and tack. As a consequence the course unfortunately changed to the northwest, as we had to cut through the growing waves at right-angles.

The convoy went past us, for we were unable to keep pace with it. We would have liked to hand over the men on the *Seeadler* to a big ship and then we would have been able to travel to the west with the convoy without a worry.

Not being able to keep up with the convoy proved fantastic luck, for they were not German ships from Kurland, but the Soviet Baltic Fleet, the so-called Red Banner Fleet travelling from Leningrad to the West to occupy the German Baltic harbours! People must have luck, especially in misfortune! But we would experience that much later.

The storm changed direction again. At 1800 hours we had to take a northerly course to avoid capsizing. It started getting dark early. The grey scraps of cloud hung down to the wave tops. It slowly became frightening. A dreadful night was ahead of us. Metre-high waves played with the *Zander* and we had no idea how to deal with them. The boat was being steered by a fine tank driver, exceptionally brave, who in all his life had never seen a motorboat before. We expected any minute our nutshell would tip over. Our dinghy, the last sheet anchor, had long since been torn away.

And the *Seeadler* hung like a lump of lead behind us. With every big wave there was a tug that shook the *Zander* to its keel. The night was so pitch black that we could not see the boat behind us. By chance we discovered that our brave little boat had a built-in searchlight. It was very calming to the nerves being able to shed a little light in the darkness. Of course, the searchlight was unable to light the way ahead in these circumstances.

The *Zander* was making hardly any progress, and the night seemed endless. Now and then we caught a glimpse of a star through the storm-torn clouds. My wide-awake senses registered every detail. Since the beginning of the journey from the Vistula I had been standing next to the helmsman without a break, helping him when I could and checking the course with my compass on my wrist and the run of the waves.

A new day, 10 May, appeared at 0530 hours, but the storm did not ease up. We were still standing at the steering wheel. All the others had crept away, and it was better that way.

I reproached myself. Perhaps I had been foolish when I had promised to take the boat over the Baltic at the beginning of the journey. Everyone on board had been seasick for many hours and were lying around unconscious. The storm turned even more against the direction we wanted to take. It was already making us go north. With the load we had in tow we simply dared not try another direction or even the slightest turn. But on this course we would never in our lives make Bornholm or even Kiel.

We had incredible luck in missing that Danish Baltic island, for the Soviets had been occupying it since 1430 hours on 9 May and only left it one year later. The German troops and refugees that had landed there were shipped off to camps in the East.

By 0800 hours the storm had become even worse. The *Seeadler* tore away, pulling a whole plank from our deck and water poured into the cabin. We tried to patch the hole in the rough seas. We had to stop it somehow. The work took hours. We worked our guts off but were determined not to drown in this roaring storm.

In the end we were able to block the leak and we hooked on to the *Seeadler* with a second throw of the grapnel. Slowly we resumed our journey, although the course was increasingly frightening. We reckoned feverishly that when this damned storm started we must have been opposite Stolp. There was nothing else we could do except cross the Baltic on a generally westerly course in sight of the Swedish coast to the east coast of Denmark. From there on it should not be too difficult to find our way home to Germany. But first, let's get away from the Soviets!

The *Zander* was making hardly more than 5km an hour. Perhaps that was good as things go. We were coming not so far from the East and the storm must blow itself out sometime. But when would that be and where would we be in relation to the land?

The helmsman was dead tired and kept falling asleep standing at the wheel. But we did not want to change places and could not do so. So went the second day in this boundless, deserted sea. We did not see a single ship. And where would we like to be? Simply away from this abominable, boiling, water-filled loneliness.

At 1915 we drove again into a raven-black third night. The sky was a little clearer but the storm continued with undiminished fury. Everything went like the previous night. We were more dead than alive. Nobody wanted anything to eat, although there were sufficient supplies aboard. The engine needed a lot of fuel. The generous supply would soon come to an end. What then? Slowly, much too slowly the time went by.

At 0800 hours the *Seeadler* tore away again, taking a whole plank off the *Zander's* deck. Water poured through the rear deck into the boat. The storm became crazy. For a large boat this was perhaps only a stronger wind, but the waves were several metres high.

There was no longer had any possibility of towing the *Seeadler*. The last grapnel had gone. We tried everything to help the despairing comrades aboard her. It took us 2 hours to come alongside the immobilised boat. Soon it was sitting like a duck on the crest of the waves, then vanishing into the grass-green boiling mass to pop up again like a cork. The propeller of our *Zander* ran for a moment in the air with the engine racing, then stopped with a sudden jolt. The steel towing rope had coiled round the propeller.

Now both boats were without power at the mercy of the raging sea. Now everything looked generally blacker for us. Most on board had long given up hope. But we did not give up, fighting bitterly against the unbridled elements. An elderly senior corporal fastened himself with a rope and tried, despite the storm and the waves, to untangle the steel towing rope from the boat's propeller. All gave a hand ensuring that we were not thrown against the *Seeadler* dancing on the waves alongside us. And despite all the gloomy predictions, the propeller was freed.

We drew our breath, listening tensely to the turmoil of the storm, listening whether now there would be a miracle, and there was. The engine started up, the propeller turned as before, the boat moved and reacted to the rudder.

But meanwhile the *Seeadler* had been driven wide off and it was clear to us that she must be abandoned. In contrast to our *Zander*, she was a big, seaworthy motor boat with ample room for twenty-five to thirty men. This boat had set off from the spit, leaving us behind like dumb idiots, with only three men on board, and we fools had already been towing these brutes for two days and two nights through the raging

Baltic. Our boat was full to the brim. Then men lay and crouched over each other. Our justifiable anger let us think for a long time about leaving the *Seeadler* men to their fate. The storm could not last forever and a boat would come by eventually. We could not be far from the Swedish coast. But our Colonel Hoffmann and Captain Illigner were aboard, and the two sailors, who would not know how egoistical the other people were.

We threw everything spontaneously into the sea, packs, washing kit and overcoats, to lighten the boat. All the boat's fittings not essential for the journey were ripped out and thrown into the sea to make room for the seven shipwrecked men. Many precious possessions that had survived the invasion and retreat from Russia sank beneath the waves. We kept only a quite light emergency pack.

Then came the risky part. We tried to get close to the *Seeadler*. It was wonderful how easily the boat manoeuvred without a tow. But it took some time before we had transferred all seven men across to the *Zander* with the *Seeadler's* raft.

Then we hauled the important fuel and drinking water across. All hands helped, forgetting their seasickness. It was very difficult in this sea and without leeway to keep our distance. We had no experience of such a manoeuvre, although we had learned a lot in the last few days. Several times the *Zander* threatened to tip over or smash against the *Seeadler*. It took hours before eventually our little boat was seven men heavier.

A well-dressed paymaster from the *Seeadler*'s crew, one of the 'anti-comrades' from the spit, had brought two fully packed giant rucksacks with him, although he must have seen us throw all our possessions into the sea in order to make room for him. He took out some delicacies that we simple front-line soldiers had not seen throughout the whole war. And this miserly chap ate them in front of us, eating all alone with good appetite and offered no one anything, displaying unbelievable lack of taste and overwhelming selfishness.

Neither had we drawn first prize with the two sailors. The lieutenant in his proud naval blue uniform, who, according to his effusive account, had travelled up and down the Baltic for ten years, puked over the steering wheel and the instrument panel. He went on to complain loudly about the damned boat, drank himself into a stupor and was of no further use to us. We were delighted when the second 'sailor', a 17-year-old ship's boy with no nautical experience, took over the wheel while he slept off his drunkenness, and we landlubbers were again left to ourselves. Our ship's boy conducted himself well right to the end, despite our reservations. Colonel Hoffmann relieved me for a while.

It was exactly 1330 hours German Summer Time when land hoved into view. Everyone jostled at the small hatch, looking for the thin grey strip that meant life for us after two terrible nights and three frightful days on this boiling sea. For us it was all the same whatever land it was. Land, and firm ground under our feet, was the what we wanted most of all. And then we saw it as a thin grey strip on the horizon. We hoped that it would be the Swedish coast, but were afraid that it might be Kurland.

A lighthouse appeared in the distance. We thought about it and, referring back to our schooldays, came to the conclusion that it must be between Öland and the Swedish east coast, which later proved to be correct. We then steered on a northerly course, keeping the lighthouse to our left. The sea was not so rough close to land, but the only thought on our mind was land, land!

We sighted a buoy and went round it three times, but could find nothing written on it. Then we steered carefully nearer the lighthouse, for there were some vast flat rocks immediately below the surface, and we had a hell of a job avoiding them. We approached the landward side of the lighthouse, where a sailor in uniform with silver insignia stood. It did us good to see a man again standing on firm ground. He made signs to us that we did not understand, nor did we understand what he was saying when we got close, but we were greatly relieved that he was by no means Russian, all breathing out great sighs of relief.

Then a motor boat with men in blue uniforms on it approached at fast speed from the bay. They too did not look Russian, and were apparently all Swedish policemen. We tried to understand each other, but it did not work out well. We could only make out that the town lying in the bay was Kalmar.

The police wanted to direct us ashore, but the four men in the boat did not look particularly friendly, especially the two older ones who looked sternly official, which did not suit us. We could not expect to get help and understanding from them. We reached a difficult decision. A younger man in the stern gave us a covert signal that we should continue our journey.

The first ecstasy had already gone. Seeing land had given us strength and hope, pulled our courage together and clarified our situation.

There was a peaceful country in front of us, but it was not Germany. We were even further from our homeland than when we left the Frische Nehrung strip. Apparently internment threatened us in Sweden. The young policeman had crossed his hands in front of his body behind the older men. Certainly the boat would be taken from us and with it any chance of escape. Perhaps we would even be threatened with being handed over to the Soviets eventually. These thoughts that were choking us for the moment meant that we would have to go back out to sea, but thus towards our homeland.

For the first time since leaving, we were not unanimous. Then the young Swede signalled to us again, clearly and unmistakably. We put the rudder over, gunned the engine and motored back out into the Baltic at full speed. The Swedish boat hesitated, but then decided not to follow us again.

We had been wise to pay heed to the young policeman's silent signal, for all those landing in Sweden or driven there were without exception gathered in internment camps and handed over into Soviet captivity at the end of November 1945.

We were still in sight of the mainland and the view of the coast was good. We felt safe. The storm appeared to have died down, and we did not regret our decision.

Fir woods and green meadows smiled across at us, and wooded promontories thrust themselves out into the sea. I had an almost irresistible desire to land on a lonely island and get my feet on firm ground. Colonel Hoffmann, who had been standing next to me since transferring from the *Seeadler*, also toyed with the thought, but we failed to find a suitable place. Sea and land seemed dead. Far and wide there were no people, no animals, no boats. The wind diminished even further. We could look down from the boat to the seabed, where large slabs of rock lay just below the surface.

We headed due south, then almost southeast, once even a little to the southwest. That this was the correct course made our hearts go faster. One of the *Seeadler* people had a map of Europe, a page torn from a school atlas with the Baltic no larger than a child's fist, but the map was of welcome assistance to us.

Meanwhile, it had become evening. The waves had faded away and we were already heading southwest. Everyone was good-humoured, all being full of hope. I sent the colonel off to sleep, having no urge to sleep myself. I was too churned up inside.

Midnight and a new day, 12 May. The swell was now bearable and we now seemed about level with Karlskrona. Away in the distance we could see a lighthouse making its silent sweep of light. My compass showed us heading west.

It began to become light at about 0400 hours. The watches were always differing, being set at German Summer Time. It was a beautiful day and the Baltic was as flat as a mirror. The Swedish mainland could be made out to the north through wisps of fog. During the night we had crossed the bight of Ystad in a straight line. The chalk-white buildings hanging like swallows' nests from the steep cliffs must be the houses of Trelleborg. A bright blue sky smiled above us. It was a truly peaceful May day, such as we had dreamed about for years.

At about 0800 hours a boat from out at sea tried persistently to catch up with us. A man on deck waved and waved, signalling with flags and a lamp, signals we did not understand. At first we thought that it must be a Soviet boat trying to get us out of the 3-mile zone, so we continued carefully closer inshore. But the people on this boat remained friendly. Then we speeded up and the other boat continued to follow.

And then we discovered something quite unexpected. The coastal waters along the Swedish coast were mined and we had been travelling through this minefield for hours. I do not know whether we had been exceptionally lucky or whether our *Zander* was of sufficiently shallow draught to enable us to travel over these devil's devices for hours without being blown into the skies. We left Swedish waters at about 0900 hours and crossed the sound, heading for the Danish island of Mön with the aid of our European map.

At 1800 hours high white chalk cliffs appeared before us. Relieved, we stared at the coast. We only knew the island of Rügen from postcards. We went along the coast for a bit, looking for a place to stop, for no way did we wish to go to Rügen. The staff paymaster swore a thousand oaths that the land in front of us was Rügen. He knew this beach well as he had spend his honeymoon on Rügen.

After all the stress we had endured, after our happy journey with its many experiences, we certainly did not want to end up in Soviet captivity. We would rather have stayed on the Nehrung spit. But we could not make any further detours for we had nearly run out of fuel. According to our map, our reckoning and consideration, this could only be the island of Mön. Why couldn't Mön have chalk cliffs around the harbour? Others were of the opinion that the chalk cliffs of Rügen were unique.

So what should we do? If it was Mön, we should go south to bypass it. On the other hand, if it was Rügen, then it was definitely time that we disappeared to the southwest before the Soviets found and arrested us.

We saw several aircraft landing on the island, which did not suit us. Then we opted for safety and sped off to the northwest. Our naval lieutenant, who had meanwhile slept off his hangover and recovered from his seasickness, had nothing to say on the subject.

Islands and groups of islands appeared everywhere, lighthouses standing on the cliffs and buoys floating about. It soon became apparent that we were hopelessly lost.

Then a fishing boat appeared ahead of us. We waved to the man on the boat but he took no notice of us. He altered course and made us understand that he wanted nothing to do with us. We were wearing black tank uniforms and he took us for God knows what. We saw that he was flying a Danish flag and constituted no danger to us.

Our fuel was almost exhausted, including that transferred from the *Seeadler,* and we could not wander about for long periods any more. We had to know for certain exactly where we were. We therefore went up to a lonely fishing boat, lay alongside and jumped on its deck. The man was alone on board and very annoyed, striking a sour tone, not wanting to understand us. But after some long appeals and many cigarettes he said that we were at the harbour entrance to Copenhagen.

So the island with the chalk cliffs had been Mön! The clever staff paymaster quickly vanished from the scene and the naval lieutenant resumed his sour, drunken attitude, and with the last of our fuel we motored on unhappily back the way we had come. Only gradually did we regain our feeling of security.

We switched off the engine at dusk, as according to human reckoning, there was still danger of running out of fuel short of our goal. We needed to get the most out of it. All slept the sleep of the just as the waves splashed gently against the boat's sides and the moon shone ghost-like through the wisps of fog. A decisive silence reigned on board.

The engine being switched on awoke me at 0330 hours. It was already 13 May. Colonel Hoffmann was standing beside the helmsman. We went back along the way we had come yesterday. At 0600 hours the familiar chalk cliffs reappeared. We drove past the south of Mön island, not liking this surly holiday resort any more.

The island of Falster appeared at 0900 hours and we took a southerly course. The German cities of Warnemünde and Rostock must be beyond our bow behind the fog, but that was where the Soviets were, so we had to bypass it.

At 1200 hours we passed the southern tip of Falster in a calm sea and beautiful sunshine. We were filled with happy hopes. We continued further on a westerly course along the southern coast of Lolland.

We left Danish waters at about 1500 hours and turned southwest towards the German island of Fehmarn. There we came across a German sailing ship flying the white flag, from whose crew we obtained much valuable information about the current situation in occupied Germany.

Somewhat later we boarded a German Coast Guard vessel that had been abandoned by her crew and was rocking on the waves. We found some soup noodles and canned meat, and cooked ourselves a wonderfully tasty, hot meal on a spirit stove that we discovered. Everyone was in the best of moods. Only a few kilometres now separated us from Germany. We were preoccupied by only one thought; seeing Germany once more. Several of the men had not been home for over two years.

A storm drew near, and the sea was visibly disturbed, but that did not bother us. We were motoring on towards peace with joyful hearts after almost six years of cruel war.

It was 13 May and the clock showed exactly 1648 hours German Summer Time when we first saw Fehmarn in the distance. Germany, our homeland, lay before us! A feeling of inexpressible joy seized all of us. Our eyes lit up. All stood on one side of the boat, which threatened to tip over, but who cared: Germany lay before us!

Destroyed radar apparatus, buried bits of iron and blown up chunks of concrete were the precise images upon our very first sight of Germany, with carefree sailors and soldiers washing themselves on the beach. We motored quite close along the shore and could not see enough of the peaceful scene here. Our joy was so great that we were thinking of going ashore here on Fehmarn. But then we came to the correct decision that we should stick to the big plans we had forged during the lonely nights. We wanted to acquire bicycles and civilian clothing in order to reach our distant homes. We wanted to go home, not make ourselves at home, and so this island was not the right place to stop.

So we steered back into the Kiel Bight. We knew that we no longer had the patience to look much further, as everything urged us to make for the mainland.

A little church tower appeared rising in the distance out of some high trees across the water. We could see people on the beach, and headed in their direction. We would have loved to jump into the water, swimming the last stretch, we were so impatient.

As the *Zander* rapidly approached the land, I had to instinctively reflect once more – five days – five nights – two unforgettably horrible nights and two lacking in hope, grey days somewhere between West Prussia and Sweden, the first glimpse of light, and then Denmark.

We carelessly ran aground close to the beach. This shocked me out of my dreams. A fisherman, who apparently had seen the impatience on our faces, quickly came up to us in his boat and helped us to get the *Zander* free again with a pole. I jumped into the water right up to my neck and waded ashore through the shallow water.

It was exactly 1816 hours when I felt firm ground beneath my feet. I had thus redeemed the promise given in distress by guiding this boat across the Baltic with, in the end, twenty-two men on board. I wanted to celebrate, I wanted to laugh and felt like crying. No shots, no trenches, no shot-up tree tops. *Peace!*

In the first moment in my overwhelming joy I could not understand why the many people on the beach were not smiling at us, why they were staring with questioning glances and anxious faces at us. And then quite gradually I found myself back in the real world. In their eyes we soldiers were only flotsam and jetsam of a lost war, sons of other parents, not their own sons that they were yearningly waiting for.

We parted from each other in individual groups, shook hands without saying much, wished each other luck for a quick return home and a new beginning. Only my radio team waited for me at the fisherman's cottage.

Under the pretext of wanting to ask the name of the place where we had landed, I went off to conceal the tears from the release of the immense pressure running down my face. I wanted to be completely alone for several minutes.

Now that everything was over, the questions instinctively sprang to mind: Why had we actually fought? Why had we had to put up with all of this? Why had so many splendid young men died? Why? Why? Why? Where was the sense?

A world had collapsed for me like a house of cards. Or was this world in which we had learned to believe in only a illusion? A mountain of questions towered in front of me and I could find no answer.

Chapter 14

After Zero Hour

In British Captivity

Heiligenhafen was the name of the fishing village on Fehmarn Sound where good fate had washed us ashore after our five-day cruise through the Baltic. Following a bit of contemplation I pulled myself together and realised I was completely alone in this situation. I threw my pistol into a deep spot in the Baltic. In front of me stretched a well-tended park with a palatial villa visible in the distance. It was the villa of the mayor appointed by the occupying powers, where I had to report, as I had been strongly advised.

I set off methodically, step by step, without thought or a plan for the future. I wandered into a landscape in which the war was dead. Then I was standing hesitantly before a massive oak door. I was admitted and bowed into a bare room.

After some time a man of uncertain age appeared who, with the modulated voice of a servant, informed me that just at this moment a Colonel Hoffmann with a Captain Dr Illigner were being taken away by two British officers, and that the head of the local community, the owner of this house, urgently advised that I report to the British; in short, that I was unwelcome in this feudal house beside the sea, where they were not prepared to even give me a drink of water, or even let me take a short rest.

I understood, and made my way with a heavy heart to the occupiers, who had assuredly been advised of my presence by the owner of the house and were discreetly waiting for me at the garden gate. The two sergeants greeted me courteously, took me wordlessly between them and that way spared me the usual demoralising 'Hands up!' and body search.

I was led, no, escorted to a nearly police post on the park wall. Two British military policemen with side arms and chinstraps and forbiddingly formal expressions took me over. After some time I was loaded into a jeep. Two young British soldiers sat in front, the co-driver with a cocked pistol held upright in his hand; a fearsome sight. We drove across a German countryside that seemed alien and unfriendly to me.

The buildings displayed British, American, French and Soviet flags. On the gable of a barn on the edge of a British tented camp was written in large letters: 'German men, loyal Germans! German women, German sows!' That was hurtful. What it meant, I had no idea at the time.

The Soviet flags were more numerous from place to place, or so it seemed to me. Suddenly I had a terrible thought: 'The British will surely not hand me over to the Soviets?' And in front of me was an unsuspecting youngster in British Army uniform, his pistol pointing skywards, close enough for me to grab. According to the Geneva Convention as I understood it, a prisoner of war was allowed to try any means of escape. So I only had to snatch the pistol from his hand with a quick grasp. I would then be able to hold the two youngsters in check without risk. I would perhaps have done it if I was certain that we were going to the Soviets – and if the two military lads had not treated me well. One can never be sure how such an endeavour would end.

It was just as well that I did not put my thoughts into action, as I was going to Plön, Montgomery's headquarters, to the new prison there. A one-man cell open to the corridor had been set aside for me. Against the doorposts were leaning two warlike English soldiers equipped with loaded submachine guns which were aimed at me.

It should be emphasised that my guards, although extremely polite and tactful, kept a distance of four paces. Their chief had expressly demanded this of them and several times warned them that they were no match in close fighting for an unarmed German front-line officer. Many thanks for this flattering evaluation!

Who apart from me was held in the prison, I would not like to say at the time. Unfortunately, I was not allowed to sit or lie on the bed, although I was dead tired. It was only now that the whole accumulated and suppressed fatigue of the last weeks came out. To avoid me falling asleep in front of them while standing, a circumstance for which they had no instructions, the two friendly British soldiers tried to engage me in conversation. They told me in detail and long-windedly what their King had told their army today, and that he had thanked the brave soldiers for their great victory.

Apparently, in their eyes I had reacted wrongly or not enough, as one of my bodyguards went off to get a newspaper, so as to give the story in black and white. In doing so he put his cocked submachine gun down in my cell. The second guard asked me if I would like to smoke. I would, although I was a non-smoker. Then he placed his weapon next to his comrade's in my safe care. I could easily have grabbed these weapons – even when the second guard returned. I had been firmly taught: 'A German officer never betrays a confidence, as every Englishman knows!'

I was given the British Army newspaper, cigarettes and matches, all at a distance of four paces as the British regulations demanded.

At about 0200 hours that night I was at last relieved of my uncertainty. I was taken through a range of security precautions for examination in a completely dark room. After the hall, it seemed it must be much bigger. What kind of special animal did the British suspect me to be?

I was stood on a precise spot, then suddenly two cruel spotlights hit me in the face. A name out of the darkness wanted to know my name, rank and unit. There was nothing objectionable in that, and I answered politely, but then made it known that, in my opinion, I had only done my duty and would only provide further information when I knew to whom I was speaking that was hiding behind the spotlights. A brief discussion followed and then the light in the room was switched on and the unpleasant spotlights turned off. The British interrogating officer introduced himself as Captain Fraser. I said that I had nothing to hide. The war was over. Of the military secrets that everyone now wanted to know, I knew none. Thereafter I was asked nothing more about them. Only our adventurous flight from Soviet custody near Danzig this way and that across the Baltic via Sweden and Denmark to Schleswig-Holstein seemed very, very doubtful to these gentlemen. They wanted to know all the details from me over and over again, repeatedly asking the same questions with different words.

Astonishingly, they already knew quite a lot, so others from the *Zander* must have been here before me. There was no other explanation, and this was comforting, for it meant that I was not alone in this prison.

Finally, I was politely dismissed with a handshake. The guard saluted smartly, despite the late hour. Speaking perfect German, Fraser apologised for the fact that he could only provide a prison cell as accommodation for the rest of the night. As a sign that I was not accused of anything, the cell remained unlocked and my two bodyguards were withdrawn in the fine British manner.

I slept the sleep of the righteous despite the prison, despite the lost war, despite the uncertain future under the well-wishing care of my relaxed guards.

I was gently woken up at about 0600 hours. One of 'my soldiers' offered to shave me. This was very painful for me, but why not? I had no shaving kit anymore, it lay in the Baltic. So I let myself be shaved by strange hands for the first and only time in my life, and was shaved superbly. The British officers' orderlies were well practised in the use of the razor. Then I was able to wash and shower, leisurely disposing myself of the accumulated dirt of the last weeks. Meanwhile 'my soldiers' had brushed my terribly tattered uniform and polished my boots. I hardly recognised myself when I saw my reflection in a mirror. But why all this? I soon found out. We were expected for breakfast in the British officers' mess, and already sitting there were Colonel Hoffmann and Captain Illigner. So my assumptions at my interrogation had been correct.

Porridge and fresh milk, eggs with ham, black tea and real coffee, white bread, butter and marmalade, sausages and ham – this was like the land of milk and honey after six years of deprivation. We ate with great pleasure and copiously. We should not have done so. I was unable to retain all this abundance, spewing like a heron and vomiting for hours.

Once we had been introduced to all this, being observed from all sides and admired for our adventurous flight, we were told that we were free and could go wherever we liked. But where in a prison surrounded by thick walls with a dozen guards?

Following a long discussion with a senior British officer, Colonel Hoffmann obtained the use of an official vehicle with a military police driver. We were unofficially informed that we were 'internees' not 'prisoners of war' and could therefore move about freely within the province of Schleswig-Holstein, which was at least a good start.

Colonel Hoffmann knew of a distant relation that lived in Sierksdorf on the Timmendorf beach, so we decided to go there. To our great astonishment, a British military policeman authorised our journey without difficulty.

The guards presented arms, the British soldiers clicking their heels together. Decorations for bravery impressed the British, even on an enemy breast, and Colonel Hoffmann wore the Oak Leaves to the Knights' Cross of the Iron Cross.

The aunt in Sierksdorf still existed, and lived in a large villa directly on the Baltic. However, the house was filled to bursting point with refugees from the East, but a small room was made available for the colonel. We two, Captain Illigner and myself, and later Lieutenant Greiner, found accommodation in a romantic holiday home belonging to a lawyer from Lübeck. We had expected quite a different kind of captivity and were especially happy. How did this compare with our comrades in Soviet captivity?

We could really move without hindrance in the vast internment area between the Elbe and the Baltic, the Trave River and the North Sea Canal. Colonel Hoffmann used this advantage to collect together the survivors of the 4th Panzer Division, as he had been allocated a vehicle by the British. He discovered the first tank men near Heringsdorf. Soon there were a few of them, then a group and then a whole company. They had got here from the mouth of the Vistula by hook or by crook.

On one of these journeys we spoke with former prisoners from Stutthof Concentration Camp, whom we had enabled to flee to the West a month before from the mouth of the Vistula – learning much, much later about all the inhumanity they had suffered.

These twice-rescued survivors told us, readily, that they together with 7–8,000 other concentration camp inmates had been accommodated on the two ships *Cap Arkona* and *Thielbec,* which, together with the *Deutschland,* were lying at anchor under white flags in the Neustadt Bight.

On 2 May they were flown over and crossed over by British bombers, but not attacked. The prisoners had formed the letters 'KZ' on the upper decks.

At about 1200 hours on 2 May the British fighter-bombers returned. The 25,571-ton *Cap Arkona* was immediately attacked with explosive and incendiary bombs and badly hit. The fire spread very quickly on both upper decks. An indescribable panic broke out as the way out to the deck was blocked by the flames, and the lifeboats and rafts had been destroyed. Only a few managed to wriggle through the portholes and swim to reach the nearby land close to Neustadt or Pelzerhaken. Of the 6–7,000 people on board only about 200 survived. The *Cap Arkona* burnt sky high. Later she tipped over and lay aground upside down, as the water there is not so deep.

At about 1430 hours the *Thielbeck* was also attacked by British fighter-bombers and torn open amidships below the waterline. She sank within 15 minutes. Of the 2,000 prisoners on board only a very few were saved.

Together with the *Cap Arkona,* the 21,046-ton *Deutschland,* which had already saved 70,000 from the East and had since been transformed into a hospital ship, was also attacked. The ship was completely unarmed and defenceless. Only eighty of the crew and some doctors were aboard, but they were able to put out the three places on fire. When the

Deutschland was flown over a second time by the British aircraft, the last lifeboat had already left. All the members of the crew, doctors and medical orderlies reached land near Sierksdorf, while the ship was so badly hit by rockets and bombs that it caught fire. Five hours later the big liner capsized.

The surviving former concentration camp prisoners declared themselves prepared to make statements to the British. As evidence they showed us the wrecks of both large ocean liners, clearly seen from the shore. The 2,815-ton *Thielbeck* was completely under the water.

Even if we did want to not fully believe this at first, the truth was soon clearly evident. For several days the tide carried the bodies of dozens of soaked corpses wearing striped concentration camp uniforms. The stench of corruption extended for kilometres.

A British colonel threw a fit, intent on convincing us of the opposite, that these dead bodies floating in the Baltic had been murdered by Germans, and demanding that we bury them. There was a big altercation between him and Colonel Hoffmann, because the latter insisted that it should first be indisputably established who had killed these poorest of the poor.

The survivors of the catastrophe stood firmly by their statements, and the people living along the coast confirmed and supplemented these, so that the true facts of the case could be established and recorded in writing clearly and unequivocally. But right up until today no one has told the world, and particularly the Germans, why the British attacked these three ships lying at anchor under white flags to the point of sinking them when ceasefire negotiations were already in progress.

Experts came from Hamburg to recover, register and bury the bodies. We were unable to observe this further, as we were ordered several kilometres inland to the village of Bujendorf, where the survivors of the 4th Panzer Division that had reached Schleswig-Holstein were gathered and organised as a company.

The rations for the soldiers caused some concern, as the British provided, per day, only six biscuits per man, and one can of corned beef for fourteen men. This amounted to only a teaspoonful each. The land around Bujendorf had been stripped bare, and there was nothing to be found. There were refugees from all over Europe, including former foreign workers that received preference for rations, as otherwise they robbed and plundered. The civilian population of Schleswig-Holstein had suddenly quadrupled, and the danger of pillaging grew every day. What people will do when they are starving!

We therefore set up a cudgel guard, each comprising two German soldiers armed with home-made cudgels guarding whatever had to be guarded: herds of cows, pigsties, individual farms and food shops. Gradually, law and order returned to the land. The farmers, who had regarded us at first as additional consumers in their village, were now happy about us and sometimes gave us wheat bran and even potatoes. This was all sold on the communal market. Apart from this things blossomed everywhere, to our delight. Dandelion leaves, sorrel and ribwort were collected by the company and mashed with the bran into a brew that could only appeal to those that had served and survived on the Russian front. We assured ourselves that this brew was healthy and vitamin rich.

We enjoyed this new life in peace immensely, and we rejoiced over our release and return home. But until it happened many things occurred and much time passed. Our impatience was put to a hard test. We thought about our comrades that had remained on the Vistula with growing concern, the unlucky ones having to face up to Soviet captivity.

Chapter 15

Ceasefire at Hela

The Hela peninsula had been like an enormous army camp for weeks, the dunes swarming like an ants' nest. On 28 April 200,000 men were counted on this narrow strip of land between the Danzig Bight and the Baltic. And every night the ferries and landing craft brought another 30,000 refugees and soldiers from the mouth of the Vistula.

Once the ceasefire with the Western Allies had come into effect at 0800 hours on 5 May 1945, all the vessels still seaworthy that had assembled in the western Baltic were sent to Hela and Kurland to take off the people waiting there. Grand Admiral Dönitz had ordered: 'Use everything possible!'

As already mentioned, on 2 and 3 May the British air force had conducted an attack on the anchored German ships in the Schleswig-Holstein Bight and sunk twenty-three merchant ships and badly damaged eight others. Thus on 5 May only fourteen transports could leave for the East, including seven destroyers and five torpedo boats of the German Navy. The armada arrived in Hela on 5 and 6 May, and by the evening of 6 May all the refugees from the Danzig area still in Hela were under way to the West, removing as many soldiers as possible from the Soviets' clutches.

During the month of April 355,624 people had been transported to the West from Hela. On 6 May alone, 43,025 refugees, wounded and soldiers left the Hela peninsula for the West. This was the highest daily tally since the beginning of the evacuation.

On 8 May the destroyers and torpedo boats evacuated another 20,000 people, mainly soldiers, from Hela under constant Soviet air attacks and artillery fire. During 8 May all the naval and merchant navy vessels headed back West, never to return.

The ceasefire conditions stipulated that no ship could leave its mooring again after 2400 hours on 8 May, and those ships still at sea should go to the nearest harbour.

The sailors had really done everything possible to bring people to the

West. It could be proved that during the last 115 days, i.e. since the Soviet offensive began, 1,977,000 German people had been transported from the East. That not everyone could be rescued was down to the conditions of the capitulation. Thus, 60,000 from Hela, 40,000 from the mouth of the Vistula and 200,000 German soldiers from the Kurland had to go into Soviet captivity.

The commander-in-chief of the German 2nd Army, General of Panzer Troops Dietrich von Saucken, was only informed by radio that the ceasefire also applied to the Eastern Front at 2400 hours on 8 May, more precisely at 0001 hours on 9 May.

Loading took place in the harbour at high speed as long as there were ships, cramming in as many as they could. The ferries, landing craft and boats that hitherto had been engaged in shuttle services between the mouth of the Vistula and Schwiewenhorst and Nickelswalde also took their last loads over the Baltic to the West.

Once there were no more boats available, when the final boat set off, unrest understandably broke out among the soldiers waiting at the harbour and among the dunes. Everyone wanted to get out of this mousetrap, and the troops broke out of the cordon.

When the commander-in-chief became aware of this at his command post, he immediately drove to the harbour. Standing up in his jeep he spoke and calmed down the thousands of disappointed men: 'We have to come to terms with it. There are no more ships available and no more expected. If we have to go into Russian captivity, then it will be with composure and in the knowledge that we did our duty to the very last.'

And the men understood him and went quietly and calmly back to their rest areas in the dunes.

On the morning of 10 May the units marched in an hours' long column past their former commander-in-chief, General of Panzer Troops von Saucken, at the exit of the Putzinger spit to the Pomeranian mainland. The Armed Forces High command had sent an aircraft to take him to Schleswig-Holstein. He had loaded it with wounded and remained behind, as he saw it his duty to share his fate with his soldiers and to accompany them into Soviet captivity. Eleven other generals went with him, but only four of them were to return home, the last in 1955.

General von Saucken, who spoke fluent Russian, was able in a personal interview with the Soviet commander-in-chief to obtain his agreement to allow the fully laden supply trucks to accompany the marching troops, for it was known that the Soviets basically provided no food for these marches. Consequently, many were spared death by starvation on their long trek to the East.

THE LAST ARMED FORCES REPORT OF THE 9th MAY 1945

From the headquarters of Grand Admiral Dönitz:
The Supreme Headquarters of the Armed Forces announces:

In East Prussia the German divisions bravely defended the mouth of the Vistula and the western part of the Frischen spit, the 7th Division especially distinguishing itself. The commander-in chief, General of Panzer Troops von Saucken, has been awarded the Diamonds with Swords to the Knights' Cross of the Iron Cross in recognition of the outstanding behaviour of his troops.

. . . Since midnight the weapons have been silent on all fronts. On the orders of the Grand Admiral, the Armed Forces have given up the pointless fight. Thus almost six years of honourable struggle have come to an end. It brought us great victories but also severe defeats. The German armed forces have finally honourably succumbed to immense superiority. The German soldier has, true to his oath, conducted himself confidently in the best commitment to his people. The homeland has supported him with all its strength and at great sacrifice. The unique conduct at the front and at home will find acknowledgement in historical judgement later. Every soldier can therefore uprightly and proudly lay down his arms and, in the worst chapter in our history, bravely and confidently go to work for the everlasting life of our people.

At this difficult time the Armed Forces think of their comrades remaining with the enemy. The dead commit us to unconditional loyalty, obedience and discipline to the Fatherland bleeding from its countless wounds.

Chapter 16

The March into Soviet Captivity

Manfred Nase, then lieutenant and commander of the 1st Company, Panzergrenadier Regiment 12, 4th Panzer Division, had to remain on the Frische spit with his men and surrender to the Soviets and their mercy and disfavour. He recorded his experience in writing:

It was the 7th May 1945 when the companies of Panzergrenadier Regiment 12 approached the landing stages at the mouth of the Vistula near Nickelswalde. We were hoping to embark during the coming night, but our transport had already gone, the ferry having steamed off full of other units. We spent the night of the 7th/8th May in a wood on the dunes near the Baltic.

On the 8th May the sun shone in a cloudless sky – precisely the kind of weather we did not want – and the Soviet ground-attack aircraft attacked without pause. Rockets exploded in the treetops and machine guns raked the sand in the dunes. It would have been very hard to have to die on the last day of the war. Surrender was mentioned for the first time. We were unbelieving for good reason, as we first wanted to get this sea journey behind us.

Late in the afternoon several overfilled transport ships left the arm of the Vistula. Then came a few smaller ships, and then it was unusually still. The planned time for our regiment had arrived, but no more ships came. All around the sea was empty, as if dead, and we feared the worst. Following a telephone call, it became clear that our situation here was hopeless.

At about 2300 hours Major von Heyden, our regimental commander, opened the sealed envelope, which finally revealed that our fate was determined in black and white. For the big majority of our men this meant Soviet captivity, if not even a senseless death.

Individuals could perhaps escape out of this trap with much

luck and even more courage. To the north lay the Baltic, and to the south, enemy-occupied land in which mainly only Polish people remained. The chances of getting out here or there were very slender.

The men in their black tank uniforms, the last of Panzer Regiment 35 under Lieutenant Grigat, nevertheless still wanted to try their luck and reported this to their combat team leader in their uncertainty. However, we moved in a very depressed mood back to the bit of woodland we had used the previous night, where we had been so hopefully happy. Parachute flares lightened the way for us. The Soviets did not trust us and wanted to prevent any flight over the Baltic.

During the night the question of what lay ahead of us bothered all crouching under the firs, and several old hands thought of the wide path they would have to retake over the Bug, the Dniepr, the Pripet, the Desna, the Oka, the Suscha until shortly before Moscow – and then even further and bloodier to here on the Vistula. And along this wide path stood the crosses of those that had fallen. Perhaps it would be better to lie there than here?

The quiet of despondency, of doubt, lay under this clear night. Only the humming of the night aircraft broke this temporarily. One watched the other to ensure that no one did something overwhelmingly stupid. Everyone had still to put their things in order in preparation for the long way ahead, the way into the unknown.

On the morning of the 9th May we saw the first Soviet soldiers, officers with interpreters, who ordered us to march off to Elbing. Going home soon, *scora domoi*, was expressly assured.

Well prepared for the march into captivity, equipped with horse-drawn wagons and supplies, Panzergrenadier Regiment 12 set off at about noon with its attached units. We still did not see any escorts. We went first towards Fischerbabke, but then diversions became necessary again, as most of the bridges had been destroyed in this watery landscape. The first night we rested at a manor farm.

We resumed our march on the 10th May, now having to be alert to Soviet soldiers looking for loot. But with our inner and outer determination we offered them little opportunity to lighten us.

On the 11th May we eventually reached Elbing. We marched singing into the town, which made a grim impression. We saw no men, not even old ones. The unprotected women and girls who had lost everything they once had, their property, their homes, their men and their womanhood, rushed out crying from the burnt-out ruins, telling us of their misfortune.

The Soviets still tried to get the few horse-drawn wagons carrying our few goods. Only with quite energetic shouts could the first be stopped for the time being.

A prisoner collecting point had been established on a sports field, and here we were searched again. We had to throw our cameras, compasses and binoculars into big barrels. Then the arriving columns were divided into blocks of about 1,000 men.

The march continued the same day towards Braunsberg. The march out from Elbing became a stirring demonstration. Our loud singing and regular marching pace resounded defiantly from the ruins. Girls and women with tears streaming down their faces threw spring flowers at us bound into small bunches. For the very last time in its history Panzergrenadier Regiment 12 marched as a formed up unit. It helped us forget our hopeless situation if comrades ahead of us, alongside us and behind us marched in step and sang the same song. We were the only ones.

Again and again we were pestered, mainly by the Soviet supply troops, who wanted their share from us. Watches, boots, medals and decorations were the most asked for souvenirs. We had to take our gunners from the self-propelled guns into the middle of us as their black tank uniforms attracted particular interest.

After two days we reached Braunsberg in East Prussia, already a well-established Soviet staging place. Here too there was no intact railway line to take us home as had been promised.

While the long column waited in front of the barrack gates of the former Infantry Regiment 21, the officers were ordered to the front. Quickly a fleeting shake of hands and good wishes, then through the wire fence on the barrack square we had another opportunity to say 'goodbye' and could clearly see how strongly the officers, NCOs and soldiers of the 4th Panzer Division had melded together during the black years. Perhaps we would not have been so obvious if it had not been for the enemy's orders for us to separate.

We remained in separate camps for several days, then our route branched off into the interior of the Soviet Union. It began a new chapter in our lives filled with bitter pain, disappointment, humiliation and death and all the costly experiences of Soviet captivity.

Chapter 17

Internment in Sweden

Erich Steinbach, then Senior Corporal in the 6th Company of Panzer Regiment 35, had the luck on the late afternoon of 8 May 1945 to be on the last convoy from Hela to the West. Circumstances obliged the naval ship taking him and forty other soldiers to Schleswig-Holstein to go to a Swedish harbour. What happened to the German soldiers interned there and eventually handed over to the Soviets to stand trial for war crimes under international law is described by Erich Steinbach in the following account:

After our Panzer Regiment 35 was disbanded for lack of tanks in Danzig at the end of March 1945, and all still combat-worthy vehicles had been assigned to the 1st Battalion, tank crews without tanks had to be released for use as infantry. With 30 other soldiers of the 6th Company, after a short training course on machine guns and panzerfausts with Field Replacement Battalion 84, I was assigned to the 3rd Company, Armoured Reconnaissance Battalion 4.

Following heavy casualties in actions on the Frische Nehrung spit and a security task at the mouth of the Vistula, we were, still as a unit, surprisingly transferred by sapper ferry to Hela, and there on the 8th May we embarked. With two comrades from our 6th Company, I climbed from the tug to which we had been assigned over to a naval destroyer. At about 188 hours this last convoy with about 60 ships and smaller craft left from Hela Harbour for the West.

As the Danish island of Bornholm appeared before us on the 9th May we believed that we were in safety at last. Then a Soviet air attack from about 30 IL-2s caught us by surprise during the afternoon. So this was how the Soviets interpreted a ceasefire. The damage inflicted was little but for this boat the aerial attack was its undoing, because our destroyer was given the task of towing an engineer ferry that had lost its power. This was not so easy in the heavy seas. The convoy had long since vanished and completely alone we jogged along through the storm with our brake in tow. And that was terrible for our stomachs; we were all seasick.

At about 2230 hours there was a powerful jolt through the ship. We were afraid that a Soviet submarine might have fired a farewell torpedo at us. But that was not so. The heavy towrope had entangled itself in the ship's propeller and we were at the mercy of the stormy Baltic without the power to move or steer. We thought we must be near the Swedish south coast. The wind was blowing from the southwest.

A Swedish destroyer stopped near us and promised help at daybreak. It returned at about 0730 hours and towed us with the engineer ferry into the harbour of Ystadt.

There preparations for our reception had, meanwhile, been made. The harbour area was fenced off with barbed wire and secured by soldiers of the Swedish Army, as we were not the only ones to come here. Another 20 German ships had sought shelter here.

Once the Swedish officers had promised us that in no circumstances would we be handed over to the Soviets, we decided after careful discussion that it would be better to be interned here in Sweden than to be in British captivity in Denmark or Schleswig-Holstein. We were to bitterly rue this decision.

On the 14th May, together with 210 other German soldiers, we were taken by truck to Malmö and from there by train to Udevalla. From there 10 trucks took us on to Backamo Internment Camp near the Norwegian frontier.

Of our 4th Panzer Division there were 25 men, 14 from the IInd Battalion of Panzer Regiment 35 and 11 from Armoured Reconnaissance Battalion 4.

The Backamo Internment Camp lay west of the big Väner Lake between some romantic cliffs in the middle of a wood and was bordered by a small bathing lake. It was a Swedish Army training camp. There were three barrack blocks, each accommodating 350 men, then there was an administrative block containing the cookhouse, and a massive brick building accommodating 120 German officers. In all there were about 1,200 men in the camp. Backamo was the largest internment camp in Sweden. It was surrounded by a triple barbed wire fence 2.50 metres high with 3 metres between the fences. There were watchtowers at every corner and vulnerable points. The accommodation and administrative buildings for the guards lay outside the barbed wire fence.

After our arrival we were registered and then allocated to our accommodation. We were given bedding, fresh clothing and the barrack schedule. Roll call was held every evening at 1700 hours and 'lights out' was at 2200 hrs.

There were representatives of all the services, submariners and fighter pilots, infantry and tank men, SS men and members of police regiments. According to the old hands, this was not a bad place. We reckoned with only a few weeks, as the war was over. The food was the best. We received the same rations as the Swedish Army and soon regained our strength.

So five weeks passed with nothing to do. In mid-June we had the opportunity of writing home via Norway, using British Field Post numbers. Just about the same time the Swedish camp commandant announced that now the time for recuperation was over and we were immediately expected to work five to six hours a day. Some aerodromes near the camp were to be extended.

The ground was stony and the work hard, but we were happy to have the diversion. The waiting time passed quicker at work. What disturbed us was the fact that we were guarded like hardened criminals. There was absolutely no need for it. Were we not all remaining willingly in Sweden?

The Swedish camp commandant inspected our efforts daily, mounted on his horse. There was nothing for him to complain about. We were able to bathe in the camp lake at a certain point. Several sailors there were able to make contact with the outside world, always returning with the latest news.

There was also a canteen in the camp, where one could buy non-alcoholic drinks, cigarettes, newspapers and toilet articles. We received pay every ten days, graded according to rank, exactly at the same rates as the Swedish Army. For staff and senior corporals this was 14 Swedish Krone. Those who did not smoke soon began to. Cigarettes were then very expensive in Sweden. We could do sport in our spare time: football, swimming and running. There were also courses in foreign languages. Every opportunity for diversion and further education was pursued.

As we could buy the Swedish and British newspapers, we learned of the monstrous crimes committed by the Nazis in the name of the German people. Now we could understand why we were guarded here like criminals. We were Germans.

We read how the state government had been deposed and Germany divided into four zones of occupation. If there was no longer a German government, who would concern themselves about us? The hope of returning home soon dwindled.

Nevertheless we prepared ourselves for the journey home. We saved our money and purchased clothing such as socks, underwear, shirts, pullovers and shoes, as we discovered from the British newspapers that none of these things were available in post-war Germany.

At the end of September we completed our task with the extension of the airfields. In the middle of October the rumour circulated that negotiations were in process for our release. At the same time we could read in the Swedish newspapers that the Soviets had asked the Swedish government to hand over the 30,000 Latvians and Estonians that had fled to Sweden and were now Soviet citizens. Also in the small print was stated that 2,600 German soldiers were to be found in internment camps on Swedish territory.

At the beginning of November the rumour spread that Swedish government had offered the Soviets the interned German soldiers in exchange for the 30,000 Latvians and Estonians that had fled.

That something was happening became clear when from the 10th November onwards no further newspapers were for sale. Even the post was held up for days.

Then came the 15th November. There was much unrest in the camp because of our concern about the future. It became known that the Soviet government had accepted the Swedish offer, and a storm of indignation broke out. The daily roll call was ignored. Everyone streamed inside the camp to the Swedish commandant's office. The Swedish colonel alerted the whole camp guard, fearing a violent breakout. But nevertheless order and discipline reigned in the internment camp thanks to our officers calling for calm. Their word still counted.

The German camp commandant was tasked, with a delegation of five officers, to speak to the Swedish camp commandant to learn exactly what was behind the rumours of our handover.

Twenty minutes later the German officers returned with the good news that the Swedish colonel had given his word of honour that he knew nothing about a handover to the Soviets. But this hypocrite and hater of Germans already knew of all the details, day and time of the handover. We had our doubts but the officers believed the word of honour of this Swedish colonel.

Next day there was a total news ban on the camp. I discussed with my two 6th Company comrades how we could break out and go to Norway. We three were not the only ones with such thoughts and had selected a suitable spot behind the rear watchtower. We were even determined to do in the Swedish sentry should it be necessary. After all the strains and perils of the long war, we were not prepared to be handed over to the Soviets like cheap merchandise.

Then came the 18th November 1945. A false calm reigned in the camp, but outside the barbed wire there was frantic activity. We could see that the guards had been reinforced. Fresh soldiers had arrived with heavy weapons and armoured cars. Now it was obvious to the optimists that the Swedish camp commandant had lied shamelessly.

On the 20th November a man returning from the hospital in Göteborg brought the news that the handover was to be on the 30th November. This date was also secretly confirmed by a Swedish sentry. A storm of protest erupted. We streamed to the camp gate with placards reading: 'Rather death than slavery!'

We debated here and there. From the beginning opinions differed widely. Finally a joint decision was reached to start an eight-day hunger strike and reject all food. The Swedish camp commandant was informed of this when he appeared at the camp gate with a suitable escort. He took the knowledge of this ultimate legitimate form of protest of the powerless and disappeared without a word.

The old camp guard, which had often treated us in a friendly manner, was dismissed and replaced by a new one overnight. Their officers had assured us that they would have no hand in our eventual handover. As an especial symbol of their unity with us, they had worn white armbands.

Meanwhile the internment camp had been transformed into a fortress bristling with weapons. A multiple security ring surrounded us. The place behind the lake that we had selected for our breakout was now additionally guarded by dogs that barked as soon as one approached the wire. A breakout was no longer possible.

Next day no one appeared for food. The food was prepared as usual. It was tipped away. We had a good supply of drinks form the canteen.

Next day the German camp administration announced that a telegram of protest would be sent accusing the Swedish government of a human rights violation if we were handed over to the Soviets. This telegram was addressed to the Pope in Rome, the International Red Cross in Geneva, the US General Patton, and the British and Swedish governments. The intent received general approval, but it could only be effective if the Swedish camp commandant dealt with it and sent our telegram on.

There was some hope, for the situation was getting increasingly more difficult for him, and the majority of the Swedish public were against our being handed over.

At the same time we decided to set up sentries at night so as not to be taken by surprise by whatever measures. The cookhouse was also guarded by us to ensure that no one broke the hunger strike.

A large medical tent had been set up outside the barbed wire perimeter with doctors and orderlies standing by. We took this as a sign that our hunger strike was being taken seriously. The first casualties occurred after five days. We waited for a reply to our telegram full of impatience, but nothing came. We took it that the Swedes had not passed it on.

We were registered once more. Everyone had to state from which place of war they had come, from East or West. We were told that men who would have difficulties with the Soviets, like the SS and police, would not be handed over.

On the eighth day of our hunger strike still nothing had happened. No reply, no reaction to our telegram. All had become apathetic, some broke down and were removed from the camp and taken away.

At noon on the 29th November Swedish police appeared in blue uniforms, specially selected men, each two metres tall, assuredly our removal commandos! We hardly slept during the night of the 29th/30th November from nervous tension, despite our exhaustion. Everyone reviewed what they still had to do in their situation. We three of the 6th Company came to no decision. One of us was for self mutilation. I was undecided, finally letting myself be convinced that it would be better to let oneself be handed over in a healthy state. We had survived so much in the war that we could also deal with whatever was to come. We had no idea that we would remain in Soviet captivity for so long.

It was, as predicted, at 0500 hours on the morning of the 30th November that Swedish soldiers marched into the camp with 200 blue policemen in front. The soldiers encircled each barrack block individually, separating us from each other and our officers. A further combined action by us was impossible. Each barrack block was surrounded by a triple cordon, each manned by at least a company. The innermost ring was formed by the giant blue policemen. Nowhere was a break-though possible.

All around there was crashing and banging. Many comrades smashed their legs with stones or cut off their toes or fingers. There was a hysterical atmosphere. My old comrade form the 6th Company hacked off two toes from his right foot. Several opened their arteries. Others stabbed themselves in the body. It was gruesome. The Swedish medical orderlies carried off all those that had wounded themselves without a word and took them to the medical tent nearby, or to the hospital in Udevalla. We too were separated from one of our company comrades in this way.

Then the blue giants entered the accommodation and each one of us was taken outside by two of them. A third came behind with our luggage. Those that did not go willingly received a blow over the head with a rubber truncheon and were dragged away.

On the barrack street stood omnibuses whose glass windows had been covered with wooden screens. Everything had been thought through and no cost spared. Once an omnibus was fully loaded, it immediately drove off, naturally under strong security precautions. The station was hermetically sealed off and surrounded with barbed wire. Four German soldiers and two Swedish guards were assigned to each compartment on the train. On every platform stood three Swedish soldiers, each armed with a submachine gun.

On the train we were amply supplied with food and drink. We did not refuse it, as the continuation of our hunger strike was now pointless. The Swedish Red Cross sisters were very sympathetic, but that did not help. By midday all the men fit for transportation, including the officers, were aboard, and at about 1400 hours the train left Udevalla station heading towards Göteborg.

The main station there was like a military camp. Apparently the Swedish population was upset and many of us had found friends in Göteborg. Even the Swedish railway men had threatened to go on strike.

We passed through Göteborg, Hälsingborg and Malmö at high speed for our destination at Trelleborg. All the stations were occupied by troops and fenced off. Civilians were not allowed in the stations when we passed through. More than a wartime division had been mobilised to cover the transportation of the 'bad Germans'.

There were three internment camps in Sweden at that time, Backamo with 1,200, Renneled with 800 and a further one with 600 German soldiers. In the Renneled Camp were many volunteers of the 11th Latvian SS Division. There things had been much worse. Several had hanged themselved and others shot themselves. Altogether there were 2,600 German soldiers in Swedish internment. 2,100 of them were transported to Trelleborg, and 500 remained in hospitals.

We arrived at about 1900 hours at the main station in Trelleborg, which again was surrounded by soldiers. Searchlight batteries illuminated the tracks and the area. For the first time Swedish military policemen took part, taking us off the train. We could only take hand baggage with us, our suitcases being loaded separately.

At the gable end of the station's big hall sat a commission of twelve Swedish officers. Everyone had to give their name and unit and then one's fate was decided. Either one left the hall on the left, or on the right. On the left meant going to Denmark and British captivity, on the right meant delivery to the Soviets. About 500 men were able to go left, being mainly sailors, airmen, SS men and policemen. A white Swedish steamer waited on the left and on the right a vast olive-green troop transport with the name *Kuban.*

A gangway had been lowered from the upper deck and on every second step stood two Swedish military policemen. We boarded the *Kuban* like a horde of hardened criminals.

On the deck were four pairs of sentries, who received us quite casually with submachine guns in their arms. We had to go below immediately and there we were searched for the first time. Knives, watches and items of value were taken from us. Then we were allocated places on the ship. It took the whole night until all 1,600 men were on board.

Next morning the Swedes delivered Swedish Army uniforms, winter coats and fur coats, and a week's ration of food. We were the very last German soldiers to go into Soviet captivity. The guards, only a dozen Red Army soldiers, behaved correctly towards us. The sailors on the ship told us that the *Kuban* would go to Pillau harbour and that we would have to do two or three months of clearing up in Konigsberg, and then we could go home. So our future did not look so bad after all.

At about 1800 hours on the 1st December the *Kuban* left Trelleborg, escorted for a bit by two Swedish destroyers. What an extravagance for 1,600 unarmed soldiers!

According to our reckoning, we should reach Pillau on the morning of the 3rd December. As we were allowed on deck from time to time for a breath of fresh air, we found that we were not heading southeast, but northeast. We had been lied to again.

On the fourth day we slowed down as we approached the coast. But where, that was the question. At 1600 hours I was on deck once more. I recognised the harbour that we were entering, it was Libau in Latvia. We had been taken from here to Danzig in January this year. I quickly ran below deck and informed my comrades, who did not believe it at first.

We stayed aboard the ship that night, and next day were taken to a camp that had been prepared for us in the docks. The *Kuban* was unloaded. The Swedish supplies, our new Swedish clothing, our cases and private belongings was all taken ashore, but we never saw any of this again with the exception of a few minor items.

The commandant of the Libau Camp, a Russian Senior Lieutenant from Moscow, who spoke perfect German, let us settle down the first day, as he knew what an upset our handing over in Sweden must have been. He told us about the camp rules, the daily roster and the camp accommodation. There was roll call every morning and evening. The menu was displayed every day. It was strongly enforced that everyone should get the allocated rations.

The days grew shorter and the first Christmas came in

captivity. All the 1,600 men from Sweden were in the Libau Camp. Rumours circulated that the Soviets did not know what to do with us and that we would shortly be released. That sounded good.

In the second half of February we were able to watch through the plank fence how the German cruiser *Niimberg* was handed over to the Soviets by British naval officers with its German crew. The German sailors were still wearing their ranks and decorations. We could only stare. After 14 days the instruction of the new Soviet crew was completed without us having had contact with the German sailors. The British naval officers returned to Germany on an accompanying ship with the German crew. We greatly envied them, although we had no idea of what stood before us.

At the beginning of March things began to happen. We were split up. Every day 100 men were taken to another Latvian camp. The roster was made according to the Russian alphabet, in which the ST with which my name began was right at the end. Consequently I was one of the last to leave Libau. With 50 other 'Swedes', as the Soviets called us because of our Swedish uniforms, I went to a camp near Riga.

There we were set to building a phosphate factory. We were promised on oath that as soon as the construction was completed we would be sent home. Yet another lie. We were taken to a camp in the Donetz Basin to another workplace. We were released from here after four whole years. I returned home just before Christmas 1949, the finest Christmas present in my life.

As a postscript, all the German soldiers that had recovered from illnesses or self-inflicted wounds that had remained in Sweden were handed over to the Soviets four months later.

These 'latecomers' told us several Swedish officers from our guard had protested about the breach of the word of honour and resigned their commissions in the Swedish Army.

Thanks should be said here, even if late, for their gesture of solidarity and all those in Sweden who wished us well.

Chapter 18

The Stars Also Shine
Over Griasovez

A Christmas Experience in Soviet Captivity by Hermann Hoss
The city of Vologda lies in immense birch woods in the north of European Russia. In the old, believing Russia it was called 'The City of a Hundred Churches in the Land of White Woods'. Today these proud churches are mainly fallen in or used as stores or stables. Only the gilded crosses still gleaming on the old green-coloured roofs shine afar in this northern woodland.

Not far from this once holy city lies the village of Griasovez, meaning 'Dirty Nest'. Traditionally it is said that the Empress Catherine had stopped here during a journey and in getting down from her coach sank over her ankles in the spring mud. Scornfully, she then ordered that the place should bear the name of 'Dirty Nest' thereafter.

In the old days devout monks founded a monastery here in the loneliness of woods and moors. As the monastery stream was attributed healing qualities for several illnesses, the holy men also built a spa that had a good name all over Russia. Apart from this, 'Russian incense' was made here. The leaves of the otherwise rare balsam poplar were collected and dried; they burned and smelt awful, and were similar to real incense from the Orient.

Of the former monastery buildings and spa only the pathetic remains still stood in 1945. The proud monastery church had been blown up in the 1918 revolution. The peasants had taken away the roof tiles to build their stoves, and what remained the Soviets had surrounded with barbed wire during the war to make a prisoner of war camp.

Since Stalingrad German soldiers had eked out a miserable existence here as prisoners of war. Already many that had died of exhaustion had been buried in the camp cemetery without ceremony.

But the war came to an end in 1945. The Soviet camp sentries called to us over the fence one May morning: 'The war is over – soon back home!'

Nevertheless new prisoners kept arriving at the camp and there was no sign of returning home. Much worse was the work spoken about, of fulfilling norms and reparation. Meanwhile the short summer passed and winter drew across the land. Winter here meant hunger, distress and also death for the people that had no special status, and therefore no preferential treatment. This all too Russian rule applied especially for the lowest on the scale in this state, namely us prisoners. Instead of the gruel soup of the summer we got daily a meagre cabbage or turnip soup. The potato mash came from frozen potatoes and smelled foul and sickly, and there were no more than two or three spoonfuls.

The cutting cold and the icy north wind burned one through the threadbare coat and the holed felt boots in the open. We huddled close together in the dark, damp huts and left them only for the most important errands. The winter also had its good side. The shortest daylight and the often raging snow storms made work in the open impossible from time to time. Thus we got more time to sleep and self-contemplation. During the polar summers with almost 24 hours of daylight we were always being driven back to work.

Only a few primitive, home-made oil lamps lightened the darkness in the huts as we dozed before the Christmas celebrations. Preparations for a joint celebration were being made in the camp. Some fir trees had been brought back secretly from work. The cooks had illegally saved a little in order to dish out better food on the feast days. Singing and music groups practised a festive programme. An artist lovingly put the programme to paper.

It could be that our Russian camp commandant, Colonel Sirma, had a loving memory of Christmas, as in other camps such celebrations were regarded as a mocking of Communism and were suppressed with all kinds of harassment.

But in the hospital, which alone came under the Soviet administration, the preparations for the Christmas arrangements were encumbered with difficulties. It was up to the German camp administration to obtain the Russian commandant's permission to hold a celebration of Christmas in the hospital. But there were other forces at work that looked on such festivities with reluctance, above all the female Russian doctor, who had been raised and brought up in the Communist spirit. She regarded the men only as matter and objects for fulfilling quotas, completely ignoring the human element.

She had already evicted many seriously ill prisoners from the hospital only because the poor chaps did not have the prescribed fever. Fever alone was the measure by which a person was gauged sick or well in the Soviet Union. The medical professionalism of this lady was as artificial as the bright red on her sensual lips.

So there was hardly any of the Christmas spirit detectable in our sickroom as Christmas Eve approached. Although some of our dear comrades had set up a decorated tree with folded paper stars, sprinkled with iodine tincture and with paper strips on the evergreen twigs. Also a light burned with thoughts of our dear home. We were also very proud of our tree and happily excited, but still more concerned about what would happen when the doctor came. And she did come.

She did not ask as usual about temperatures, appetites and stools, but headed straight for the Christmas tree with an unfathomable look. The pairs of eyes from us sick followed her with imploring, almost hypnotic power. In the silent room the tension between two differing wills was almost palpable.

Scorn blazed in the Russian girl's eyes and she lifted her foot as if to kick the tree over. But our gaze forced her to turn around and the eyes gave her the strength to walk away. Her face twitched briefly, she then made a derisive gesture with her painted lips and rushed out of the room. A heavy load fell from our hearts.

None of the sick comrades were chased out of the hospital that day and our fir tree now stood upright as our Christmas tree. Suddenly our hearts were seized with a happy Christmas feeling, which became even more profound when we received permission to write our first Red Cross cards home that Christmas Eve 1945, informing our loved ones that we were still alive. With homemade pens, with ink of potassium permanganate solution, happily excited we scribbled the few words allowed.

That evening we celebrated our Christmas undisturbed in the hospital. A priest came from the camp with two violinists and gave us the message about the birth of the Lord. Two thin violin voices swept through the wretched room and transported us away from sad reality. Thus we hardly noticed a white doctor's smock had entered our room. Not the one with lipstick this time, but the wife of the director of the nearby flax mill – we called her the 'flax woman'. She was a good soul with a human heart, who had already helped a few of the sick within the limits of her ability. She was also older, and had experienced the religious Russia.

She stood almost unnoticed among us, her eyes lowered at first curiously and then transfigured by the wretchedly decorated tree and the lips of the priest telling us the Christmas story. Although she understood only a little German, one could see in her eyes that memories of childhood were rising strongly within her and were taking a powerful hold of her. When broken voices joined the violins in 'Stille Nacht, heilige Nachl', she covered her eyes with both her hands and a stream of tears poured between them.

She swayed, sobbing convulsively and pressed us foreign, poor, hated German prisoners of war in our shirts and underpants by the hand and kissed us on our sunken cheeks as was customary in old Russia. We looked on deeply moved. To us it seemed as if we had experienced a Christmas miracle in this country so foreign to us.

As the song died down the 'flax woman' darted off, but with radiant eyes. For hours we no longer felt the cold coming through the cracks, our misery and the unspeakable loneliness. We directed our gaze and our thoughts at the ice-starred window to the West, towards our homeland. Never had the stars shone so light and brightly over Griasovez as they did that Christmas Eve of 1945.

Timeline

12 Jan. 45	Marshal Zhukov's 1st Byelorussian Front attacks from its bridgeheads south of Warsaw towards Posen and Pomerania.
13 Jan. 45	The 3rd Byelorussian Front attacks East Prussia heading for Königsberg.
14 Jan. 45	Marshal Rokossovsky's 2nd Byelorussian Front attacks the 2nd German Army from the Narev-Bug Triangle, heading for the mouth of the Vistula.
20 Jan. 45	Soviet soldiers cross the German border near Hohensalza.
23 Jan. 45	Soviet tanks force their way into Elbing.
25 Jan. 45	The German Navy and Merchant Navy begin the transport by sea of refugees from Pillau, Danzig and Gdingen.
27 Jan. 45	Strong Soviet units reach the town of Tolkemit on the Frisches Haff, breaking the land connection to East Prussia. The Red Army crosses the Vistula near Mewe, 60km south of Danzig.
30 Jan. 45	The *Wilhelm Gostlof* is sunk by a Soviet submarine near Hela at 2200 hours. Of the approximately 5,000 on board only 937 are saved.
01 Feb. 45	The Red Army reaches the Oder near Küstrin.
02 Feb. 45	Thom Fortress is lost, the garrison consisting of the 73rd and 31st Infantry Divisions breaks out and heads for the German lines.
05 Feb. 45	The Soviets take the Kurische Nehrung.
10 Feb. 45	At 0050 hours the German hospital ship *General Steuben* sunk by a Soviet submarine. Of the 1,476 severely wounded, 1,213 walking wounded and 900 refugees, doctors, nurses and crew, only 630 are saved. The town of Elbing is lost.
13 Feb. 45	The town of Schwetz is lost.
15 Feb. 45	Tuchel and Schneidemühl occupied by the Soviets.
18 Feb. 45	Konitz lost.
24 Feb. 45	The city of Posen occupied by the Soviets.

28 Feb. 45	Schlochau in Hinterpommern is lost.
03 Mar. 45	Red Army troops reach the mouth of the Oder at Stetttin.
05 Mar. 45	Soviet troops reach the Baltic coast in Pomerania, cutting the German 22nd Army off from the homeland, re-supply being only possible by sea.
08 Mar. 45	The Soviets occupy Stolp and Stolpmünde.
09 Mar. 45	Marienburg, which has been surrounded by the Soviets since 25 Jan., is evacuated.
10 Mar. 45	The German Navy engage in the land fighting in the Danzig Bight with the ships *Prinz Eugen, Schlesien* and *Leipzig* for the first time.
12 Mar. 45	The town of Karthaus evacuated. Dirschau on the Vistula is lost. General von Saucken takes over command of the German 2nd Army.
13 Mar. 45	The Soviets reach the Danzig Bight near Putzig, breaking the land connection with Hela. Neustadt and Schönwalde fall to the Soviets. Refugee transports from Danzig and Gdingen reinforced. Marshal Rokossovsky's 2nd Byelorussian Front's five armies attack towards Danzig and Gdingen.
13–15 Mar. 45	Construction of a line of defence on the high ground west of Danzig and Gdingen.
20 Mar. 45	Soviet attack between Zuckau and Ramkau following three-hour long bombardment.
23 Mar. 45	The Soviets take Zoppot, splitting the Danzig bridgehead into three. The divisions of the 2nd Byelorussian Front launch a main attack on Danzig following an extraordinary bombardment.
24 Mar. 45	Marshal Rokossovsky calls on the soldiers of the 2nd German Army to surrender.
25 Mar. 45	As this appeal is ignored, Danzig is bombarded and smashed. The last German transport *Ubena* evacuates the last of the refugees from Danzig's Neufahrwasser harbour.
26 Mar. 45	The suburb of Oliva is lost.
27 Mar. 45	Langführ is abandoned without a fight. General Betzel, commanding the 4th Panzer Division, is killed at the Oliva Gate in Danzig. On the orders of the 2nd German Army, the sluice gates on the Vistula dykes are opened and the dykes breached

	by German engineers, flooding the Elbing meadows to protect the troops as far as the Frisches Haff.
28 Mar. 45	The western part of Danzig has to be abandoned to the Soviets.
	The Mottlau Line is to be held until the troops and refugees have moved to the wooded dunes by Heubude.
29 Mar. 45	End of the battle for Danzig. The German troops withdraw over the Vistula.
30 Mar. 45	Danzig lost. The last German rearguards leave the city on the night of 29/30 March.
31 Mar. 45	The 2nd German Army orders the destruction of all vehicles, except those of the 4th Panzer Division.
04 Apr. 45	Oxhöft immediately north of Gdingen evacuated, the last German troops leaving at 0600 hours on 5 Apr. 45.
05 Apr. 45	Withdrawal of front line to behind the arm of the Vistula near Neufähr.
10 Apr. 45	Königsberg city lost.
16 Apr. 45	Liner *Goya* sunk off Rixhöft by a Soviet submarine. Of the 7,000 aboard only 183 saved.
23 Apr. 45	An attempted landing by the Soviets near Neutief rejected by Armoured Reconnaissance Battalion 4.
24 Apr. 45	Major von Heyden's armoured group deployed in the area from Kahlberg to Liep.
26 Apr. 45	Heavy casualties in blocking fights from Kahlberg to Steegen until the beginning of May.
1 May 45	Narmeln on the Frische Nehrung lost.
2 May 45	Berlin fully taken by Soviets.
3 May 45	The Royal Air Force sinks twenty-five German cargo ships and damages eight others in the Lübeck and Kiel Bights.
5 May 45	All cargo ships still available head for Hela and Kurland to evacuate the soldiers still fighting there.
	Pröbbernau taken by the Soviets.
	Ceasefire with the Western Allies from 0500 hours.
7 May 45	The evacuation of all refugees from Hela completed. Evacuation of troops begins.
8 May 45	Announcement of ceasefire in the East. From 0001 hours on 9 May on all fronts.
10 May 45	100,000 German march in orderly fashion into Soviet captivity. The last of these return home ten years later in 1955.